BIG GUNS

Casemate Short History

BIG GUNS

ARTILLERY ON THE BATTLEFIELD

Angus Konstam

CASEMATE

Oxford & Philadelphia

Published in Great Britain and
the United States of America in 2017 by
CASEMATE PUBLISHERS
The Old Music Hall, 106–108 Cowley Road, Oxford OX4 1JE, UK
1950 Lawrence Road, Havertown, PA 19083, USA

© Casemate Publishers 2017

Paperback Edition: ISBN 978-1-61200-488-4
Digital Edition: ISBN 978-1-61200-489-1

A CIP record for this book is available from the British Library

Printed in the Czech Republic by FINIDR, s.r.o.

For a complete list of Casemate titles, please contact:

CASEMATE PUBLISHERS (UK)
Telephone (01865) 241249
Email: casemate-uk@casematepublishers.co.uk
www.casematepublishers.co.uk

CASEMATE PUBLISHERS (US)
Telephone (610) 853-9131
Fax (610) 853-9146
Email: casemate@casematepublishers.com
www.casematepublishers.com

CONTENTS

INTRODUCTION

THE DISCOVERY OF GUNPOWDER LED TO the creation of a weapon capable of fully devastating force. For the next seven centuries this weapon – the artillery piece – would evolve from being little more than a battlefield novelty into one of the most deadly weapons in mankind's arsenal. Artillery was once a status symbol of monarchs eager to display their state's wealth and power. As the 'black art' of gunnery evolved into a science it became a military necessity – the means by which armies could capture fortresses, or secure a military edge on the battlefield. Artillery became the cornerstone of the technological revolution that transformed both ships and naval warfare, and more than any other weapon it reflected the great inventive achievements of its age. This, though, led to artillery pieces becoming the ultimate killing machine of the industrial age, whether in the batteries massed behind the trench lines of World War I, or arming the great battleships that symbolised the fusion of destructive firepower with technological achievement. Artillery was the key to victory in two world wars, and even today it remains a potent force on the modern battlefield. This is its story, a 700-year tapestry of invention, technological breakthroughs, industrial ingenuity – and deadly intent.

C7th	Use of 'Greek Fire' by the Byzantine navy.
C10th	First recorded use of gunpowder weapons by the Chinese.
1241	Mongols may have used gunpowder weapons at the battle of Mohi, the first use of this technology in Europe.
1326	First written evidence of the use of artillery in Europe.
c.1380	Venetians use cast-iron balls, and mounting bombards in their galleys.
c.1509	First gunports on warships.
1515	Battle of Marignano – history's full-scale artillery bombardment on a battlefield.
1537	First Western artillery treatise, Nicolo Tartaglia's *La Nova Sciento Invento*.
C16th	First development of indirect fire mortars and howitzers.
C16th/17th	Fortifications redesigned to resist artillery, culminating in the designs of Vauban.
1618–48	Thirty Years War. Gustavus II Adolphus divides his artillery train into field guns and siege guns.
Late C17th	Cartridges begin to be used rather than loose powder, speeding up loading.
1693	French army establish a permanent regiment of artillery.
c.1700	Invention of grenade throwers and more effective howitzers.
1756–63	Seven Years War. Frederick the Great forms batteries of horse artillery.
1765	Gribeauval artillery system approved by Louis XVI of France.
1803	Shrapnel shells adopted by the British army.
1837	Paixhans guns firing explosive shells enter service in France.

1840s	Royal Navy starts to use 68-pounder smoothbore shell guns.
	Percussion system of ignition adopted for artillery use, later replaced by friction primer system.
1850s/60s	Adoption of Beaulieu rifled muzzle-loading guns by the French; Armstrong rifled breech-loading guns (RBLs) by the British; and Krupp rifled breech-loading guns by the Prussians.
1865	Development of first type of smokeless gunpowder.
1877	French produce the De Bange 90-mm, the first modern breech-loading gun.
1880s	Development of time fuses for shells; armour-piercing rounds; and Quick Firing guns.
1897	The 75-mm Quick Firing Gun enters service with the French Army.
	Development of accurate sighting devices improve accuracy.
1905	The launch of HMS *Dreadnought* transformed naval warfare, ushering in the 'Dreadnought Era'.
1914–18	World War I. Development of rolling barrage, box barrage. Development of the first tracked artillery transports, and anti-aircraft guns.
1916	British and German navies clash at Jutland, the only full-scale naval battle of the war.
1939–45	World War II. Development of armour-piercing discarding sabot (APDS) rounds, and high explosive anti-tank (HEAT) rounds. Invention of radar enables sophisticated fire control systems.

CHAPTER 1

MEDIEVAL ORIGINS

14th – 15th centuries

WE ALL KNOW THAT ARTILLERY CAME to be a battle-winning weapon – 'the queen of the battlefield' or 'the god of war'. This though is a modern idea, born a century ago amid the blood and carnage of World War I, when hundreds of guns pulverised enemy trench lines before the infantry went 'over the top'. Even then it was a notion more than 600 years in the making. When artillery first made its appearance it was seen as little more than a novelty – a toy for princes to play with. Back then, those who created and fired these strange new weapons were seen as practitioners of a 'black art', not unlike alchemy, medicine, and witchcraft. Everything though, has to start somewhere, and artillery quickly emerged from its misty origins to become first a reliable military weapon, and then a crucial part of any self-respecting army. This journey was a tricky one, with more than a few wrong turnings along the way. Even today historians disagree where the road actually began. What follows is the most commonly agreed version of the way artillery was first invented, and how it developed.

The first guns

In September 1325, at Altopascio in Tuscany, the Florentine army was soundly defeated on the battlefield. The Florentines dug deep into their coffers to raise and equip another force to defend the city, and the ledgers listing this great outlay still survive. Hidden in one dated 1326 is an entry that shows that medieval Florence was at the cutting edge of military technology. It records the appointment of gunfounders, hired to produce bronze guns for the Florentine arsenal, together with the iron balls and arrows for them to fire. This is the earliest written evidence for the use of artillery in Europe.

This confusing reference to arrows is easily explained thanks to a pair of English illuminated manuscripts. They were produced in 1327 by Walter de Milemete, the chaplain to King Edward III. Both of their illustrations show small bulbous guns shaped like a vase, sitting on a trestle table. In the manuscripts they were described as a *pot de fer* (iron pot). In each picture, a mail-clad gunner is shown firing the weapon by applying a piece of burning rope or even a red-hot poker to a small touchhole. From the mouths of these guns a large harpoon-like arrow can be seen. Halfway down its shaft a ball of rope or cloth was wrapped round it, to hold the arrow firmly in the pot, and to seal the mouth of the gun. Clearly this was the projectile, waiting to be fired by the gun at the enemy. These medieval illustrations show some of the world's first ever pieces of artillery. Crude though they were, these guns, and those that followed them, would transform the face of warfare.

They were fired using gunpowder. This is a combination of three ingredients – saltpetre (or potassium nitrate), charcoal, and sulphur. While the recipe changed with the telling, the ratio used to make modern 'black powder' for fireworks or the firing of replica weapons is roughly seven parts of saltpetre to one part of the others (7-1-1). The saltpetre acts as an oxidising agent, while the other two are forms of fuel. The combination is a volatile explosive mixture, which burns extremely quickly when set alight. As it does so it generates a large amount of heat,

A pot de fer *(early artillery piece), an illustration from the illuminated manuscript by Walter de Milmete entitled* De nobilitatibus sapientii et prudentiis regum, *c.1326. (Stratford Archive)*

light, and gas. Someone then had the idea of compressing this gunpowder into a small open-ended metal chamber, then setting it alight. They discovered the explosive blast was directed out of the open end of the chamber. By plugging the open end with a projectile, they found this was blasted out with shocking force. This metal chamber therefore became the first gun.

Oriental origins

Quite where guns and gunpowder were invented remains a mystery. In the 19th century some historians claimed that gunpowder weapons were first invented in antiquity, citing a passage written by the Roman historian Livy that mentioned a machine invented by Archimedes which 'with a terrible noise did shoot forth great bullets of stone'. Similarly, a much earlier Sanskrit code of laws suggested that the Indians of pre-history used gunpowder weapons. Both of these, and other similar claims have long since been discredited. They referred to mechanical weapons, not firearms, and a combination of poor translation work by antiquarians and a lack of understanding about old projectile weapons led to the confusion.

Much more credence can be given to the claim that the Chinese were the inventors of gunpowder weapons. As early as AD 940, Chinese chronicles describe the use of 'fire lances' in battle. Most historians now believe these were probably a form of flamethrower, fixed to the end of a bamboo pole – one that used gunpowder to work. Effectively, these fire lances were the forerunners of the modern firearm. In 1044 an even clearer description of them is found in a manuscript which speaks about explosive fire lances. Soon imperial workshops were created, solely to produce gunpowder weapons for the state, while the production of gunpowder was also a state-run industry. Clearly the Chinese were leading the world when it came to firearms.

Chinese used larger gunpowder weapons too. In the 11th century, Chinese weapons described as large 'eruptors' were used to launch projectiles at the enemy, 'capable of killing a man or horse', and could even 'transfix several persons at once'. While there is no clear reference to guns or gunpowder here, it was obvious this was what they meant. By that time the Chinese were mining potassium nitrate in near-industrial quantities from the caves in the Laojun Shan Mountains, in Sichuan province. Eleven gun foundries in Liao Dynasty China were kept busy creating weapons that would transform the Imperial Chinese army, while in 1067 – the year after the battle of Hastings – the Liao Emperor Daozong prohibited the export of saltpetre and sulphur. The Liao Dynasty wanted to keep this new technology out of the hands of both rebels and the barbarians beyond the Great Wall.

Relief carvings in Sichuan dating from the mid-11th century show the use of both fire lances and rocket-launched arrows. By the 12th century larger gunpowder weapons were being used by the Jin Dynasty against Chinese rebels, while in 1232 the armies of the Emperor Aizong used artillery to recapture cities during their doomed counter-offensive against the Mongols. Following the overthrow of the last Jin emperor and the seizure of the Imperial throne by Ogedai Khan (son of Genghis Khan), the

Mongols gained access to this new technology, and the weapons that came with it. The Mongols probably used gunpowder weapons during their later campaigns in Europe. While these may have been limited to flaming arrows and naphtha bombs, some claim that it was the Mongols who first introduced gunpowder to Europe.

Of course, flamethrowers and naphtha weren't new to the west. The Byzantine navy had used the flamethrower known as Greek fire in the 7th century AD, while in the mid-14th century, at the time of the Mongol invasions, Muslim troops were using naphtha weapons against the Crusaders. These were fire weapons though, rather than explosive ones. If the Mongols had indeed used gunpowder weapons against the Hungarians at the battle of Mohi (1241), then this could have been the first use of this Chinese technology in Europe. Certainly, despite the attempts of the Mongol emperors to limit the spread of gunpowder the Koreans were using it by the start of the 14th century, while in the same century gunpowder weapons were being produced in the Arabian peninsula. This diffusion of technology is reasonably evident from the historical record. What remains unclear though, is how and when the use of gunpowder first developed in Europe.

Introduction into Europe

Certainly the English Franciscan monk Roger Bacon (*c.* 1219–92) knew about gunpowder in 1267, as he described it in his *Opus Majus* (Greater Work), which he presented to Pope Clement IV. It has been suggested that the Oxford-based academic encountered it from another Franciscan, who brought a sample back from his travels in the Mongol Empire. Others suggest Bacon created the mixture of saltpetre, charcoal and sulphur himself, and tested it with explosive effect. Claims that Bacon produced a gunpowder recipe have proved misleading, as the proportions he recorded in cypher would have been virtually non-combustible. Still, it was clear he knew of gunpowder's dramatic properties. Wherever its origins, it was clear that gunpowder – if not gunpowder weapons – had reached Europe by the time Bacon wrote his book.

Claims that artillery was used by King Henry III of England during his campaign to restore royal authority in the 1260s are misleading, as the term encompassed siege engines, which fired solid spherical projectiles, or even incendiary ones. Even this use of incendiaries is unlikely. The Church disliked the idea of Christians waging war against each other when there were hordes of Muslims and Mongols to fight. So, to limit the scale of warfare it banned the use of such weapons within Europe. This might have temporarily curtailed experimentation with gunpowder, but it certainly didn't stop it. *Liber Ignium* (*Book of Fires*), a collation of recipes for incendiary mixtures written around 1300 included notes on the gathering of saltpetre, and recipes to make gunpowder. The genie was out of the bottle.

The existence of the late 14th-century German monk Berthold Schwarz is doubtful, as no record of him exists. It is just as likely he was invented by later scholars to provide a Germanic origin for the development of gunpowder. By the time he was supposedly carrying out his alchemic experiments, guns and gunpowder had been in military use for almost half a century. That account of guns being used in Florence in 1325 was merely the first of a growing number of instances where gunpowder weapons appear in the historic record. It was claimed that guns were used by Germans at the siege of Metz (1324), and by the Moors at the siege of Baza near Grenada the following year, but no contemporary records survive. Jean Froissart's *Chronicles*, written in the later 15th century, mention both 'bombards' and 'cannon' being used by the French at the siege of Le Quesnoi (1340), but in the contemporary French accounts these terms aren't found – only the much more dramatic name *tiaiux de tonnaire* (tubes of thunder).

Waterstones

Bank Hey Street
Blackpool
FY1 1QN

01253 296136

SALE TRANSACTION

PRE-PAYMENT   -£7.99
200006601575
Item Refunded - Customer Order Deposit
BIG GUNS   £7.99
9781612004884

No items 1
Balance to pay

£0.00

WATERSTONES REWARDS POINTS
WATERSTONES REWARDS POINTS WOULD HAVE
EARNED YOU 23 POINTS TODAY
ON ITEMS WORTH £7.99
Apply now at thewaterstonescard.com

VAT Reg No. GB 108 2770 24

STORE TILL OP NO. TRANS. DATE   TIME
0208   1   781371 233702 27/06/2017 11:39

9990202080012337026

If your Kindle is faulty we will replace it when returned within 30 days. For those returned after 30 days but within the manufacturer's warranty period, we will gladly arrange a replacement from the manufacturer.

This does not affect your statutory rights.

Waterstones Booksellers,
203/206 Piccadilly, London, W1J 9HD.

Get in touch with us:
customerservice@waterstones.com
or 0808 118 8787.

Buy online at Waterstones.com or Click & Collect. Reserve online. Collect at your local bookshop.

Did you love the last book you read? Share your thoughts by reviewing on Waterstones.com

Waterstones

Refunds & exchanges

We will happily refund or exchange goods within 30 days or at the manager's discretion. Please bring them back with this receipt and in resalable condition. There are some exclusions such as Book Tokens and specially ordered items, so please ask a bookseller for details.

If your Kindle is faulty we will replace it when returned within 30 days. For those returned after 30 days but within the manufacturer's warranty period, we will gladly arrange a replacement from the manufacturer.

This does not affect your statutory rights.

Waterstones Booksellers,

Then, in the accounts of the Flemish city of Bruges for 1339, there is a mention of a *ribaudequin*, which from Froissart we learn meant a light gun, three or four of which could be mounted together on a small cart, called a *char de guerre* (war cart). Then, at the battle of Crécy (1346), Edward III reputedly used a handful of *pots de fer* to help him win his battle against the French. They would have been of little tactical use, but he probably deployed them for their psychological impact rather than their potency. Next, in 1353, in the stores records of the Tower of London, is a mention of just such a group of royal guns. In Latin, the record states that four copper guns, 16 pounds of gunpowder and one copper mortar and iron pestle were stored there. In this period, 'copper' really means bronze. A further note claims that the guns were made by William of Aldgate, and cost 13 shillings and 4 pence apiece. Could these have been the very guns used by the king at Crécy?

These four guns were still there when the next inventory was made seven years later. However, by 1365 there were 11 bronze guns in the store, two of which were described as 'large'. Clearly then, not all guns were the same. Despite the term *pot de fer*, only the projectile was iron – the pot itself appears to have been bronze. Both its shape and the need to contain the blast necessitated the use of this stronger metal. These small *ribaudequins* (ribaudekins) and *pots de fer* were only the start. Even larger bronze guns now made an appearance. How then, did these differ from the two French guns made by Ramundus Arquiero of Toulouse in the mid-14th century, described as 'iron cannon', and supplied with lead shot and leather-covered wedges? Guns were now appearing in a variety of sizes, and made from both bronze and iron. What did they look like?

The *pot de fer* was simply a vase-shaped container made from bronze, with a touchhole at the end. The mouth of the vase was around 2–3 inches (50–75 mm) in diameter, into which was placed the projectile – usually an iron arrow, bound with leather so it sat securely in the mouth – or muzzle. From a surviving example excavated at Losholt in Sweden we know that the base was thicker than the rest of the pot, to help absorb the blast. The whole thing was laid horizontally to fire, strapped to a table or trestle. Experiments have shown that the arrow could be fired with reasonable accuracy for a few hundred yards. However, the bang caused by the combustion of the gunpowder was impressively loud. This supports the notion that the pot's main use was to strike fear into the enemy.

Ribaudequins were probably little bigger than later medieval handguns, but appear to have been made from iron. However, there is little hard evidence to base this on, apart from a surviving example from Perigord in southern France, which probably dates from the 15th century. It had a dozen barrels, which could be fired off in groups of three. Unlike the iron pot though, when mounted on wheeled carts these small gun batteries were fully mobile, which made them useful on the battlefield. Finally there were the larger guns – the *cannons* and *bombards* mentioned by Froissart, of the kind reportedly built by the contemporary gunfounder Arquiero of Toulouse. These though, were probably made using wrought iron. Bronze gunfounding technology was in its infancy in the 14th century, and was carried out by founders used to casting church bells rather than weapons of war. They had no knowledge of the power of gunpowder, unless they learned from trial and error, and survived the process.

Building large bronze guns was therefore problematic, unless they were little more than large versions of the *pot de fer*, like the two stored in the Tower of London in 1365. For big guns, iron was the material of choice. The way this was done was to build a barrel using wrought-iron bars with angled edges, like the staves of a barrel. These were grouped around a wooden core, until they formed the shape of a tube. White-hot wrought-iron hoops which were marginally wider than the tube were then hammered over the staves, until the tube was completely covered by them. As the metal cooled they would form an even tighter fit around the staves. So, when the wooden core was removed, what you were left with was a heavily reinforced iron tube, open at both ends. This became the barrel of the gun. This method was known as 'hoop and stave' construction.

There were two ways to turn this barrel into a weapon. One would make it a muzzle-loaded gun, the other a breech-loaded one. In the former, a thick cast-iron disc was inserted over one end of the tube, usually by plugging the end hole. This though, was a weak point in the design – if the gunpowder blast was too large, the end piece could be blown from the gun. This was a risk the builders were willing to take, as ballistic power imposed a constraint on the size of a breech-loading gun. A breech chamber sat at the end of the gun, and was held in place using wooden blocks and wedges, or by having its own slot in a wooden gun carriage. It contained the powder and shot, and when the charge was ignited the projectile would be blasted through the barrel towards the target.

The weak point of this design was the seal between the powder chamber and the barrel. If it wasn't tight enough gas would leak out when the gun was fired, lessening the explosive power of the weapon. It was also dangerous if a gunner was caught unawares. The breech (or powder) chamber varied in size depending on the size of the gun. Small ones would be little bigger than a beer mug, forged from wrought iron. Larger ones needed four men to lift it into place. The larger the gun then the greater the likelihood of gas escaping through the breech. Larger still and the chamber would be too heavy to move. So, for the largest bombards, muzzle loading was the preferred option.

The great bombards

In 1375, Jehan le Mercier was ordered to build 'a grand cannon of iron' in Caen for the French crown. He hired three master smiths, who set about forging over a ton of wrought iron. The long staves were fused together by heating and hammering them,

A late medieval ship, armed with small guns. The Ship of St. Stonybroke,
by unknown artist, woodcut, c. 1490. (Stratford Archive)

and then the heated rings were hammered in place. Rope was
used to wrap the iron barrel, and then a skin of leather hide was
stitched over the top, to make the whole thing weatherproof. As
no mention is made of either an endpiece or a powder chamber,
it is unclear whether this was a muzzle-loading or a breech-
loading weapon, although its evident size suggests the former.

Two years later, in 1377, the Duke of Burgundy had a bombard
built with a 22-inch (55-cm) bore, capable of firing stone round
shot (cannonballs) weighing over 440 pounds (200 kg). This was
a truly devastating weapon, and was first used in anger at the
siege of Odriuk that same year. This though, was only the start.
Less than half a century later another Duke of Burgundy owned
a gun called *Dulle Griet* (Mad Margarite), which fired balls twice
as heavy as this earlier bombard. Also, unlike its predecessor,
it fired cast-iron round shot, making the projectiles far more

deadly. These were first heard of in 1380, when the Venetians used bombards firing cast-iron balls to batter the walls of the Genoese-held port of Brondolo, near Chioggia. They proved highly effective – much more so than stone round shot or iron arrows. So, by the end of the 14th century, guns had developed from mere novelties into potentially powerful weapons of war.

As well as providing them with siege guns, the Venetians embraced artillery for another reason. The city's commercial power was based on maritime trade, supported by a powerful Venetian navy. The fleet was composed of oared galleys, which relied on ramming, archery and boarding to win a sea battle. During the War of Chiogga (1378–81) fought against the Genoese, the Venetians upgraded many of their larger galleys to carry a bombard, mounted in the bow, on the centreline of the galley. This proved a battle-winning stroke, giving the Venetians the firepower to sink enemy galleys with a single shot. Soon other Italian maritime powers like Genoa, the Papal States and Naples followed their lead, and naval warfare in the Mediterranean took on a whole new dimension.

Gunpowder might have originated in China, but it was Europe where artillery developed rapidly into a major military arm. The reason was largely instability. In China the emperor retained control of both gunpowder production and gunpowder weapons. As a large central power the only threat to his realm came from internal rebels or external raiders, who for the most part lacked the resources and firepower of the imperial army. So, there was little impetus to develop artillery. By contrast Europe was divided into a patchwork of rival kingdoms and states, and war between them was commonplace.

For instance, the Hundred Years War (1337–1453) pitted England against France, although inevitably other neighbouring countries were often sucked into the conflict. In Italy, rivalry between the city states often led to open warfare, while the emerging Duchy of Burgundy came into conflict with the city states of Flanders and the Low Countries. The patchwork of states that made up the Germanic Holy Roman Empire were often feuding with one another, while further east the same empire faced religious unrest in Bohemia, while the German military orders were locked in a bitter and seemingly endless struggle against the peoples of Eastern Europe. This all meant that Europe was in near-constant military ferment. So, in order to gain an edge over its rivals, rulers and civic leaders turned to guns and gunpowder to give them a martial edge. In turn this demand for ever more powerful guns led to the rapid technological development of artillery during this period.

Certainly the power of this new generation of artillery was easily demonstrated. In 1405, Henry IV of England used a siege train to help quell a rebellion by the Earl of Northumberland. In short order he reduced all of the earl's strongholds, including near-impregnable Warkworth Castle, which surrendered after just a few shots from the king's bombards had brought down part of the castle's outer walls. A decade later in 1415 the king's son, now Henry V, used twelve great bombards to besiege the French port of Harfleur. They battered a breach in the city's wall, and Harfleur surrendered. While Shakespeare has Henry storming the breach, yelling 'Once more unto the breach, dear friends, once more; Or close the wall up with our English dead,' in fact there was no need, as the royal bombards had already done their job and forced a capitulation.

A pair of English breech-loading bombards from this period can be seen on Mont St. Michel off the Brittany coast, left there when the English abandoned the castle in 1424. These powerful wrought-iron guns are both 12 feet long, weighing well over a ton, with an 18-inch bore. In both guns the 3-foot-long powder chamber has survived, as have the stone round shot they fired, although any carriages or wooden beds have long since rotted away. These were exactly the kind of guns Henry V used at Harfleur – crude, powerful, and effective. Still, they were relatively small compared to some of the bombards that followed them. Six years later in 1430, James I of Scotland imported a great bronze bombard called *The Lion* from Flanders, a breech-loader reputedly capable of firing a ball weighing 500 pounds. Bombards had now become national status symbols, where size was everything.

We have already encountered *Dulle Griet*, built in Ghent in 1430, with its 25-inch bore. Guns of this size were now too big to effectively use as conventional breech-loaders. Their powder chambers were becoming too big to remove easily between each firing, and more importantly the powder they required now placed an inordinate strain on whatever arrangement of wooden beds, carriages and wedges held the chamber in place. So, the Flemish designer who produced *Dulle Griet* came up with a novel solution. Both the chamber and the end of the barrel had a screw thread, and one simply screwed into the other. Slots in the chamber allowed wooden staves to be inserted to help unscrew the chamber. This absorbed the blast far more effectively, and made the gun safer to operate.

This was necessary for another reason. Around the middle of the 15th century the nature of gunpowder changed. Before that, the saltpetre, charcoal and sulphur had been ground up and mixed together. These often separated out when stored, so barrels were frequently turned, or the powder mixed. It was also highly susceptible to the damp. Then came corned powder, which was made by taking gunpowder that had already been ground and mixed together, then dampening it before grinding and crushing it again, this time into a finer powder. This 'corned' powder was then sieved to produce an extremely fine 'serpentine powder'. It was found that this was far more volatile than untreated powder – and therefore more explosive. Consequently guns using serpentine powder were placed under greater pressure, which in turn increased the risk of a barrel bursting, or more likely a powder chamber being blown loose. So, it was used with caution.

This finely ground gunpowder proved more useful for handguns with their smaller powder chambers than larger guns, but where artillery really benefited was from priming. When a gun was fired, a powder trail leading through a touchhole into the powder chamber was ignited using a burning piece of sulphur-impregnated cord known as 'slowmatch', or by placing a red-hot poker to it. The finer the powder the easier it was to ignite, and therefore the more reliable it became in setting off the main charge. So, from the later 15th century on, while coarser powder could be used for the main charge, finely ground powder came to be used as priming powder for artillery.

Meanwhile guns were continuing to evolve. The tendency to produce increasingly large bombards continued throughout the 15th century, although from 1425 bronze guns began to appear, such as the bronze bombard bought by James I of Scotland. Bronze is essentially an amalgam of nine parts of copper mixed with one part of tin. It was reasonably easy to cast using the same technology used to cast bells, and this technology had improved greatly during the late medieval period. Now, hardened bronze was far tougher than the wrought iron commonly used to produce bombards. From the 1440s, bronze became increasingly

Mons Meg *at Edinburgh Castle. (Alamy)*

popular in gun foundries, particularly for the production of larger guns. After all, it appealed to rulers who wanted to flaunt their artillery train as a status symbol, demonstrating that their guns represented the latest word in gunfounding technology.

Still, wrought-iron guns continued to be used for another century. The great wrought-iron bombard *Mons Meg*, which still sits on the ramparts of Edinburgh Castle, was built in Mons around 1449, and then sent as a gift to James II of Scotland by the Duke of Burgundy. Its builder was Jean Cambier, gunfounder to the duke, and was presented to the Scottish king in 1454. It was 9 feet long, or 15 feet with the powder chamber in place, and weighed around 3 tons. It had a bore of 20 inches, which meant it could fire a stone ball weighing almost 400 pounds. Unlike the slightly larger *Dulle Griet*, the powder chamber was slotted into the end of the barrel, and then bound permanently in place using thick iron bands, which made it a muzzle-loader. Like many bombards of the period it lacked a carriage – the current one supporting *Mons Meg* is an 18th-century invention. Instead, a wooden bed for it would have been built at the siege lines, and the gun set on it and wedged in place.

James II was a keen advocate of artillery, but it proved his undoing. In 1460 he laid siege to Roxburgh Castle, on the Scottish Borders, which was held by the English. He brought along his siege guns to bombard the castle, and *Mons Meg* was probably one of these. Also present was a bombard called *The Lion* – possibly the same bronze gun imported into Scotland by the king's father 30 years before. During the bombardment the wooden bed supporting *The Lion* broke under the strain, and the breech chamber and its metal wedges blew out of the back of the gun. One of these pieces struck the Scottish king on the thigh, severing his leg. It was a mortal wound, and he died where he fell, beside his beloved guns.

This increasing tendency to build large guns using bronze wasn't merely a Western European development. The Ottoman Turkish Sultan Mehmed II the Conqueror shared James II of Scotland's enthusiasm for artillery, but had infinitely more resources at his disposal, as well as his own gun foundries. He built up the Ottoman Turkish siege train into one of the largest of its day. At the siege of Constantinople in 1453 a total of 70 guns battered the walls of the Byzantine capital, including 19 large bombards. One of them was reputedly so enormous that it fired a stone ball weighing 1,500 pounds. If this were true, this made it the largest bombard in existence. The Byzantines placed their faith in their city's formidable defences, but these were unable to deal with the ferocity of what was probably the first large-scale artillery bombardment in history. In less than two months the city's huge walls were breached, and the last bastion of the former Roman Empire fell to the Turks.

A surviving bombard of this period illustrates how the Ottomans were at the leading edge of gunfounding technology during this period. 'The Dardanelles Gun' was presented to Queen Victoria during a state visit by Sultan Abdülaziz in 1868, and now forms one of the key attractions at Fort Nelson, the national museum of artillery near Portsmouth. This great bronze bombard was cast in 1464 by Munir Ali, gunfounder to Mehmed the Conqueror, and while a beautiful object in its own right, bearing Turkish decoration and inscriptions, it is also remarkable for its construction. It was cast in two parts, with a breech section taking up a third of the 17-foot-long gun. The two parts were joined by an impressively engineered screw thread, which provided an extremely tight seal. The 17-ton gun had a 26-inch bore, and fired a stone ball weighing 676 pounds. Remarkably it was still in use in the early 19th century, mounted in a fort guarding the entrance to the Dardanelles. In fact, in 1807 it fired on British warships as they tried to force their way through the strait.

Medieval mobility

While these great bombards might have been spectacularly effective when it came to knocking down a castle wall, they were incredibly difficult to transport. They needed lifting apparatus to hoist them on and off carts, which in turn needed dozens of draught animals to pull them. Dozens more were needed for all the accoutrements – stone or metal round shot, wood and tools to make the bed, tools to operate the gun, gunpowder to fire it and ideally a forge, so the gunners could make running repairs in the field.

The transport of even a moderate siege train was an enormous undertaking, especially as many of the main roads in late medieval Europe were little more than tracks. There was no alternative, save to transport the guns by sea wherever possible. That though, wasn't always practicable. There were two solutions to this. The first was to create guns that had a similar destructive power to the bombard, but which were lighter. This inevitably meant the creation of large, powerful bronze guns, which might fire a smaller ball than a bombard, but which had far greater hitting power. The second saw the development of what we now call the gun carriage. These already existed for *ribaudequins* and other small guns. Now this mobility would be made available to all guns.

In fact, by the mid-15th century guns already came in a variety of sizes, from the *ribaudequin* up to the great bombard. An English poem of the late 1450s mentions 'bombards, serpentines, fowlers, crappaudes, culverins and other sorts'. Our understanding of these terms is helped by contemporary records, which flesh out some of the details. The 'fowler' was a large, heavy breech-loading wrought-iron gun – effectively a smaller version of the breech-loading bombard. It was also called a 'bombardelle'. The gun was usually mounted on a carriage of sorts, and was also used at sea, where these guns were sometimes called 'murderers'. The 'crappaude' was a 'curtow', a smaller, more portable version of the same weapon, while 'serpentines' and 'culverins' were smaller still, but had long barrels and a narrow bore. While this is confusing to us, it was just as perplexing to contemporaries, as often different terms are used for the same type of gun.

In the 16th century the culverin became the name for one of the largest types of gun, while in 1474 Duke Charles 'the Bold' of Burgundy had seven serpentines in his siege train, all 8–10 feet long apart from one much larger piece, which fired a ball twice the weight of its fellows. In a Tower of London inventory of 1495, the storekeeper listed 21 guns, three serpentines, and equipment for bombardelles, curtows, demi-curtows, serpentines, falcons, small serpents, and hackbuts. Among this confusing nomenclature is a useful list, giving the weight of shot of some of these guns:

Gun Type	Weight of Shot
Bombardelle	263 pounds
Curtow	100 pounds
Demi-Curtow	40 pounds
Serpentine	6 pounds
Falcon	1 pound (lead)

This and other similar inventories tell us that gun types were becoming increasingly varied as the 15th century drew to a close, but essentially all guns were still divided into large siege guns and smaller pieces, breech-loading weapons and muzzle-loaders, and finally bronze and wrought-iron guns.

It is fortunate for us that in 1474–75 Charles the Bold suffered a string of defeats at the hands of the Swiss, and many of his captured guns can now be found in Swiss museums. What is remarkable about them is not the range of guns but their carriages, recorded by the Swiss, and illustrated in contemporary Swiss manuscripts. They show two-wheeled carriages for many of the guns, with the guns set into their wooden beds or carriages. Others were mounted on three-legged trestles, looking a little like a machine-gun tripod, while other larger bombards sat on flat wooden beds. Clearly the Duke – just as keen on artillery as James II and Mehmed the Conqueror – had already considered the problem of mobility, and made his artillery as portable as he could. Little could be done with the heaviest of guns though. A Burgundian document of 1474 states that it took 24 horses to pull a large bombard, but just eight for a curtow, four for a serpentine and two for smaller pieces. While this was hardly a fast-moving force, at least it was a mobile one.

The sheer pace of change is surprising. Artillery first appeared in Europe in the 1320s. While the first guns were simple affairs, within little more than a decade the first major variant appeared – the *ribaudequin*. This small, portable gun, mounted on a wheeled carriage became the forerunner of the mobile artillery pieces of a later age. Then, less than half a century after the first small *pot de fer*, large wrought-iron bombards were appearing – guns with sufficient firepower that they could demolish a castle wall with a few well-placed shots. These merely got bigger as gunfounders and their patrons became ever more ambitious. This, of course, meant that guns became increasingly immobile, so the next step was to develop guns which could accompany an army on the march. By the end of the 15th century, as the renaissance of European culture and ideas spread throughout the continent, and as European explorers ventured further afield, artillery was about to undergo its own transformation, turning gunnery from a mystical 'black art' into a science worthy of this brave new age.

CHAPTER 2

THE RENAISSANCE

16th–17th centuries

IN 1494, CHARLES VIII OF FRANCE led an army across the Alps and into Italy. At the time France was the most powerful state in Western Europe, but Charles had just inherited the Kingdom of Naples, and was determined to lay claim to his new dominion. At the time Italy was fragmented into dozens of little states, and so at first this French invasion was virtually unopposed. This changed the following year, when an anti-French league was formed, and the French army was forced to withdraw. They would return though, and for the next two decades Italy would serve as the battleground between the French king and the Holy Roman Emperor, whose territories included Spain and Germany. The Italian states switched sides as the political pendulum swung between the two foreign powers. While the arrival of a professional French army in the peninsula came as a shock to the Italians, what really surprised them was the mobility of the French train of artillery.

This shouldn't have been so unexpected. After all, Charles the Bold had been developing mobile artillery pieces two decades earlier, and thanks to their experiences in the Hundred Years War the French had moved away from bombards, and now favoured smaller and more mobile guns. The Italians though, still favoured larger bombards, and had little experience of mobile field artillery. These French guns were much lighter, much more mobile, and thanks to their well-thought-out designs, they were more accurate. Since the mid-15th century the French crown had been developing state gun foundries, the largest of which was at Lille. They in turn drew on expertise from Flemish gunfounders, and by the 1460s their guns were as technologically advanced as any in Europe.

In the 1460s, these medium-sized French guns were fitted with trunnions – projecting lugs attached to the gun barrels. These allowed a gun to be easily elevated and lowered on its gun carriage, which in turn made aiming them much simpler. The result was an improvement in accuracy. The first trunnions took the form of lugged sleeves slipped over the barrels of existing guns, a little like one of the rings on a wrought-iron gun. Later, these trunnions were cast as an integral part of a bronze gun. Effectively, this development was closely related to the increasing use of gun carriages – one was designed to be used with the other. Interestingly, most of Charles the Bold's guns lacked trunnions, even though his Flemish gunfounders were purported to be the best in Europe. It seems it was the French who now led the way, both in gun design and in mobility.

Other French improvements included the abandonment of stone round shot – they relied entirely on cast-iron balls – and the development of a new generation of powerful bronze guns. Essentially these were designed to replace the bombard, and again, while these came in a range of sizes and calibres, and a bewildering array of names, they all shared certain characteristics. This new generation of artillery was cast from bronze, with trunnions roughly midway along the barrel, mounted slightly below the centreline of the gun to make it easier to elevate the piece. They were muzzle-loaders, with the barrel ending in an integrally cast cascabel, or rounded end. The bore was much smaller compared to older bombards although the gun length was often the same, which meant these guns were more slender than their predecessors. Their barrels were bored out rather than built up, so the shot fitted snugly inside them, meaning that the shot was fired with a greater velocity.

This, and the altered ratio of gun length to bore size generally made these new bronze pieces far more accurate than older bombards, or even wrought-iron guns of the same size. When they were mounted on a carriage that permitted easy elevation and aiming, and relatively easy mobility around the countryside, then these guns truly represented a major step forward. Inevitably, these French and Flemish designs were quickly copied by other states. For instance, Holy Roman Emperor Maximilian I had his gunfounders in Augsburg and Nurnberg develop guns of a similar style, as did Henry VII of England, whose new guns impressed a Venetian diplomat who toured the Tower of London in 1497. So, as a new century dawned, a new generation of guns was appearing in foundries all across Europe.

In 1504, the keeper of Maximilian's arsenal recorded how his new German guns fell into several categories. First there were the *Hauptbüchsen,* or siege guns, a category which encompassed all of the old large bombards. Then came the more modern heavy bronze guns, which were given an assortment of names, but all of which were also used as siege pieces. Next came the *schlangen* (culverins) and *basilisks*, the more mobile medium guns which could appear on a battlefield. Here the length of the barrel was at least twenty times the width of the bore. Finally came the peculiar pieces, such as multi-barrelled organ guns (descendants of the *ribaudequin*) and mortars, which were also used as siege pieces. While the terms would change, this general division in terms of function and size became commonplace across Renaissance Europe.

Machiavelli once wrote that Italian artillery of the late 15th and early 16th century was pulled by oxen, and usually arrived too late for a battle. Even if they did turn up, then he claimed they rarely fired more than a shot or two before the two armies clashed. By contrast a contemporary bas-relief celebrating France's victory

The late 16th-century Pavensey Gun, mounted on a replica carriage, Pevensey Castle. (Malcolm Fairman/Alamy)

at the battle of Marignano (1515) show French guns on their own gun carriages, pulled by teams of horses, keeping pace with the army as it advanced. This was why the more mobile artillery of the French made such a strong impression on contemporary Italian chroniclers. This though was nothing compared to the impact these guns had at the battle of Ravenna, a battle fought between the French and a joint papal and Spanish army. The Allied army was protected by formidable earthworks, defended by dozens of guns.

The French countered this by massing a battery of more than 50 guns, and for the first two hours the battle took the form of an artillery duel. After silencing the Allied artillery the French guns kept pounding the defences, before the French commander launched an all-out assault. As a result, the French infantry captured the defences after a brisk fight, and so won the battle. This was probably history's first example of a full-scale artillery bombardment on a battlefield, and it offered a clear demonstration of just how far artillery had come since its first appearance on the European battlefield – it was now a weapon that could win battles. Artillery also proved its worth at the battle of La Bicocca in 1522, when the Italian guns eviscerated the Swiss pikemen – then the toughest mercenaries in Europe. This also demonstrated that the French no longer enjoyed a monopoly of good-quality modern artillery. In fact, three years later at the battle of Pavia (1525), the entire French train of artillery was captured by the Imperialists, following their assault on the French siege lines around the city.

Siege guns

This increase in the use of artillery on the battlefield was matched by other developments. The first had really begun in the early 15th century, when the new generation of bombards showed just how vulnerable castles were to artillery fire. There was little that could be done with most existing castle walls, as they were too high and too thin to offer much of a challenge to a well-sited bombard. So, either the walls were thickened, to better absorb the pounding, or else additional walls were built in front of them. Ideally, artillery defences were low and thick, and earthworks were better than stone at soaking up a bombardment. In some key places, specially constructed artillery forts were built, with suitably robust walls, and with defensive guns of their own. A prime example of one of these forts is Southsea Castle outside Portsmouth, built to defend Portsmouth Harbour from attack by land or sea.

During the 16th and 17th centuries the old medieval walls surrounding European cities were often ripped down to make way for new defences, designed to counter the new threat posed by artillery. Key towns were now surrounded by low, thick walls that sloped outwards at an angle to reduce the power of incoming shot. Gun towers dotted these walls, housing artillery pieces ready to fire at an approaching enemy. The next development

Mid-16th-century siege guns, from The Siege of Munster, *a woodcut by Erhard Schoen, c. 1536. (Stratford Archive)*

was the *Trace Italienne* (Italian Trace), a triangular bastion with stone walls which stuck out beyond the defensive walls. So, even if a besieger's guns blasted a breach in the walls, attackers storming the breach would be caught in a murderous cross-fire from the flanking bastions.

The real master of this kind of military architecture was the Seigneur de Vauban, who served Louis XIV of France as a military engineer. He built more than 300 fortifications around France during the later 17th century, and as the foremost military architect of his day his name was used to describe the best and most skilfully constructed defences of the period, where geometry was used to make these 'Vauban' fortifications as impregnable as possible. This was becoming increasingly necessary, as new types of artillery were being developed specifically to lay siege to new scientifically designed fortifications.

Mortars were one of these new weapons. The mortar had a short, wide barrel, and used a relatively small powder charge, but rather than firing a projectile directly at a target it was designed to lob a ball high into the air. It would then drop onto the top of an enemy's defences, or behind them, into the town they were built to protect. Early mortars fired solid projectiles – stone or cast-iron round shot. Then, from the mid-16th century mortars began using explosive bombs, and in 1588 the first of these were used in action at the siege of Bergen-op-Zoom in Flanders. Essentially, these were the first effective explosive shells. Another new development was the howitzer. These were guns that could fire indirectly, like a mortar, but they could also fire directly at a target in front of them, like a conventional artillery piece.

Mortars and howitzers were specialist siege weapons, but the bulk of a siege battery would be made up of large and powerful bronze guns, whose job was to repeatedly batter the same stretch of wall until it collapsed, creating a breach that the besieging infantry could then storm. These siege guns were the largest and heaviest guns of their day, and while they might be difficult to transport on campaign, their effectiveness was unquestionable. So, both guns and forts were being developed during this period, one to counter the effectiveness of the other. This struggle for supremacy would continue for centuries – in fact it can still be said to be continuing today.

The use of wrought-iron breech-loading guns continued into the 16th century, but they were fast being replaced by more powerful bronze guns. During the 16th century major gun foundries sprang up around Europe, to serve this growing need for high-quality ordnance. While Liege, Lille and Augsburg remained the largest of these throughout this period, other smaller gun foundries also thrived, and European museums contain prime examples of their work. By the mid-16th century the art of gunfounding had reached a technological plateau, where the essentials of the production process were now well-established, and would continue in the same vein for another 250 years. Even the basic design of these guns themselves would remain largely unaltered – the only real differences were superficial – the current fashion of the age when it came to gun size and decorative embellishment. In other words, artillery had finally emerged into the modern age.

One thing that did change though, was the type of metal used. Bronze was the material of choice because it was hardy and reliable; its only real drawback was its cost. So, from the early 16th century some founders tried producing guns using cast iron, but these proved unsuccessful as the metal itself wasn't strong enough. This changed in the mid-16th century when new casting techniques meant that cast iron became tougher and more reliable. In 1543, the first successful cast-iron gun was produced in Buxted in Sussex – a village at the heart of one of Europe's largest iron-working areas. Soon cast-iron guns were being produced in quantity, first for use at sea, then for shore defences, and finally for armies. The appearance of reliable cast-iron guns proved the death knell for wrought-iron pieces, which rapidly gave way to these new cast weapons. However, for prestige, reliability and ready availability, bronze guns maintained their dominance well into the 18th century.

This of course was the period known as the Renaissance, a cultural and intellectual movement which encouraged science, learning, discovery and artistic endeavour. The military world was caught up in this great movement, which manifested itself in new weapons and tactics, and in military thinking. The 'black art' of gunnery was an obvious area where a more scientific approach could pay dividends, both through improved gunfounding technology, and in the way guns were designed and used. The result was the publication of the first artillery treatises, whose aim was to transform the art of gunnery into a science. The first of these was *La Nova Sciento Invento*, written by the Venetian mathematician Nicolo Tartaglia in 1537, and dedicated to Henry VIII of England. It advocated a more mathematical approach to ballistics. This was ground-breaking, as it revealed just how a gunner should aim an artillery piece in order to hit a distant target. Tools such as a quadrant marked in degrees were now vital elements in the new-found science of gunnery.

In 1588, Tartaglia was translated into English, and published together with an appendix written by Cyprian Lucar which covered the duties and responsibilities of a gunner. It advocated a sober, inquisitive approach to the job, and emphasised the need to master these scientific skills. Another crucial treatise was

CASTING A GUN

To produce a cast-bronze or -iron gun the founder began by making a full-sized model of the piece using a wood pole, wound with rope and then with a layer of clay coated over the top of it. At this stage there wasn't a breech end – that would be added later. Wooden replica of the trunnions were pinned in place, along with wax replicas of any lifting handles (often taking the form of dolphins) or other decoration. Then, the surface was greased before more layers of a harder type of clay were added to form a cocoon around what was now a full-scale replica of the gun. This outer clay layer would form the mould for the piece. The whole thing was then bound in iron hoops to hold it together during the metal pouring stage.

Once this was all done the wooden spindle would be pulled out, along with any of the rope, with the clay stuck to it, and the wooden trunnion formers. When this was finished the mould would be hollow, but bearing the impression of the finished gun on its inside surface, like a sort of negative replica. In other words, this process was all about making a full-sized clay cast of the gun. The breech end was moulded separately, and this was now attached to the end of the gun mould. A greased iron spindle was then inserted into the mould, and held in place using iron spacers called chaplets. It was crucial that this was exactly centred in the mould, or else the finished gun would have an off-centre bore, and would therefore be useless. The mould was then taken to the casting pit.

Here it was carefully set upright, ready for the metal pouring. Sometimes several guns were placed in the pit at the same time. The pit was then filled with dampened earth, to hold the moulds in place. The furnace would have been heating molten bronze (or iron) for some time, and by the day of casting it was white hot. The furnace would be tapped, and the liquid metal was directed along channels leading into the top of the gun moulds. The actual casting part of the process was relatively quick. Once the metal had cooled the moulds were excavated from the pit, and then carefully broken open, revealing the finished cast gun inside them. At its muzzle the pouring had left a sprue of metal, called the bloom.

This was sawn off, revealing the iron core inside the barrel. This was carefully removed too. The gun was now taken to a vertically mounted boring machine and the bore was drilled out. The iron core had established the size of the gun's bore – this last stage ensured no burrs of metal remained inside the gun, and that the bore was both smooth and of exactly the right size for the shot the gun would use. All that was left to do now was to drill out the touch-hole, and to test fire (or proof) the piece. That done, the gun was ready for service.

Vannoccio Biringuccio's *Pirotechnia*, published posthumously in 1540. This Italian scholar's book explored metallurgy and the explosive force of gunpowder inside a gun barrel. In other words, his was the first study to scientifically look at the way guns were designed from a metallurgical standpoint. This result was a better understanding of gunfounding, and the production of more reliable guns.

William Bourne's *The Art of Shooting Great Ordnance*, published in 1578, also advocated a scientific approach, but tempered with the pragmatic knowledge gained from experience. Bourne also set out a list of gun sizes and calibres, as had Tartaglia and Lucar. While these all revealed a gradual move towards a standardisation of gun types and sizes, Bourne was clearly basing his on his practical experience as a gunner. A similar approach was adopted by another Englishman, Robert Norton. In his treatise called *The Gunner*, published in 1628, he added the weight of his extensive experience in the form of a dialogue about gun design, gunpowder and ballistics. This was a really practical handbook for gunners who wanted to learn about their trade. Taken together, these treatises really transformed the nature of gunnery and gunfounding, and encouraged a new sense of professionalism in the black art turned science.

Several of these treatises provided a categorisation of guns, usually listing them by shot size and weight. While the terms changed during the 16th and 17th centuries, the general trend was for clearer divisions in terms of gun size and shape, as well as in the size of shot these guns fired. Older gun types such as the bombard, the bombardelle and the serpentine had largely disappeared by the mid-16th century, and within a few decades so too had curtows and port pieces. These terms only appeared in inventories, listing older guns in storehouses such as the Tower of London. In the field, or on board ship, large guns tended to be bronze or cast-iron muzzle-loaders, divided into a handful of categories. Muzzle-loading guns only remained as small swivel pieces, which remained in use, albeit in declining numbers, throughout the period. The trend was towards fewer categories, and greater standardisation.

The following list comes from John Smith's *An Accidence*, published in 1626:

Gun	Weight (pounds)	Shot size (inches)	Shot weight (pounds)	Powder charge (pounds)
Cannon	8,000	7¾	63	46
Demi-cannon	6,000	6	32	24
Culverin	5,500	5	18	14
Demi-culverin	4,500	4	9	9
Saker	3,500	3¼	5¼	5¼
Minion	1,500	3	4	4
Falcon	1,100	2½	2¼	2¼
Falconet	500	2	1¼	1¼

While the weight and bore of guns varied slightly from table to table, and some versions included further subgroups such as cannon royal, cannon of 8 inches, cannon of 7 inches, bastard culverin, culverin drake or robinet, these were merely attempts to cover every size and shape of gun in use. The term 'bastard', for instance, covered a gun that didn't conform to the standard proportions of its calibre, while a 'royal' was a slightly larger version of the normal cannon. A 'drake' tended to have a tapered bore, and was a little lighter than the norm, while a 'robinet' was even smaller than a 'falconet', with a bore of about 1½ inches. Today the term cannon is used to describe any gun large enough to need a carriage. In the Renaissance, it was a far more specific term, describing only the very largest pieces of ordnance.

While these terms can appear confusing, there was a logic there, as all guns of a particular category tended to be roughly of the same size and shape, and so could be told apart from guns in other categories. One other appellation of the period was 'perrier', which was used to describe guns originally designed to fire stone shot, but which now fired shells or grenades as well. These tended to be shorter than regular muzzle-loading guns of the same category, and often had a tapered powder chamber, but fired the same diameter of shot. The cannon perrier, for instance, was 8 calibres (or bore widths) long, which for a gun with an 8-inch bore made it 5 feet 4 inches long.

These classifications though, were fairly broad ones, and the gun sizes and weights listed tended to be averages. Individual guns might vary slightly in length, weight, bore size and shot weight, but were still grouped together into one general category. In the early 16th century the term culverin was used to refer to the group of guns that were proportionately longer in relation to their bore size than cannon, thereby producing a longer, slimmer-looking gun. All the other smaller classes tended to follow its proportions – in other words they were all of the same family in terms of appearance. It also meant that cannons had different proportions, giving them a squatter and less elegant appearance, but also a more deadly one.

These guns all had to be mounted on carriages, and by the mid-16th century these tended to be of similar construction. The barrel sat between two pieces of timber, known as cheeks. These resembled thick planks stood on their side. The cheeks were usually spaced apart using three transoms, at the front, middle and back of the carriage – known as the breast, bed and trail respectively. A few inches back from the front of the carriage semi-circular slots were cut out of the cheeks, to house the trunnions of the gun itself. Beneath the cheeks, a little forward of these trunnion slots an axle was bolted to the underside of the carriage. It tended to be square in the centre, but round on the ends, to allow the fitting of a pair of carriage wheels.

The cheeks tended to be reinforced with iron bands and bolts, as was the join between the carriage and the axle. The gun itself rested on the trunnion slots, with the breech end of the gun resting on the bed. A pair of semi-circular iron cap squares were fitted over the trunnions and attached to the cheeks, to hold the gun in place. At the trail end a hole in the transom allowed the pintle of a gun carriage to be hooked on to the gun, while rings attached to the trail and the cheeks were used to either manhandle the gun, or to secure it to a limber. This style of gun carriage varied a little over time, but essentially it remained in use for the best part of 400 years.

At first, naval carriages were similar. Then, by the time the *Mary Rose* sank in 1545, a new type of naval carriage had evolved, where the cheeks were thicker and shorter than on a land carriage, and joined together by a continuous bed, rather than by three transoms. These cheeks had trunnion slots, just like a land carriage, but behind this were a series of steps, which meant the back of the carriage was almost as low as the stool bed. Instead of one axle there were two – at the front and back – and rather than being fitted to spoked wheels like a land carriage, solid wooden truck wheels were used. These were better designed to operate in the confined space of a ship's gun deck. Interestingly, in the Spanish Armada campaign of 1588, the Spanish sea carriages resembled land ones, while the English used these new truck-wheeled carriages. The Spanish found the English guns were better handled and could be reloaded far more quickly than their own pieces. Incidentally, these same truck-wheeled carriages were used for guns in fortifications throughout this period.

So, by the 17th century the evolution of artillery into a scientific force was well underway. While there were few technological changes during the century – just minor changes in gun dimensions and appearance – the real change came on the battlefield itself. During the Thirty Years War (1618–48) Gustavus II Adolphus of Sweden divided his artillery force (or artillery train) into field guns and siege guns. Effectively, all guns which fired shot weighing more than 12 pounds became siege guns. Lighter guns – demi-culverins, sakers, minions and so on – became field guns. That way his more mobile artillery could move at the same speed as the rest of his army, rather than wait for the lumbering heavy guns. This built on the already existing idea of a 'train' of artillery, where all the guns, equipment, powder, shot and trained gunners were grouped together into one homogenous force.

His other innovation was to design 'leather guns'. Despite their name these were metal guns, albeit with lightweight barrels made from copper, which were then bound with rope before a leather sleeve was sewn over the top of them. Similar guns were used by the Scots during the English Civil Wars. These were small, light guns, and when mounted on equally small and lightweight carriages they were mobile enough to keep pace with the infantry during an advance, and so could use their firepower at close quarters. While these guns weren't particularly effective in terms of firepower or accuracy, they did help introduce the concept of 'regimental guns' – small artillery pieces of minion size or less, designed to fight in direct support of an army's infantry rather than be grouped with bigger guns in more static gun batteries. One of the battlefield problems of the day was that gun batteries were usually masked by friendly troops as the infantry advanced. This way the infantry could still enjoy the support of artillery fire.

Gustavus Adolphus was one of the first European rulers to move away from the old nomenclature of guns. In his army, guns tended to be categorised by the weight of shot they fired – 6-pounders, 12-pounders, 24-pounders for instance, rather than sakers, demi-culverins and culverins. While this was an idea ahead of its time, the idea gradually gained acceptance as the century wore on. By the late 17th century, the old names had largely fallen into abeyance. Around the same time the use of cartridges came into vogue, where rather than ladling loose powder into the barrel of a gun, re-measured bags of powder were inserted instead. Not only was this safer, but it greatly speeded up the process. In *The Gunner's Glasse*, published in 1646, Master Gunner William Eldred wrote that siege guns now had a rate of fire of around eight rounds a minute. Smaller field pieces could be fired at roughly twice that rate, and lighter regimental guns could be fired more frequently still.

However, Eldred warned that after about 40 shots the barrel needed to be cooled for an hour, to reduce the risk of accidentally igniting powder inside the red-hot barrel. He also advocated that gunners take their trade seriously, learn the mathematics that underpinned accurate firing, and generally adopt a thoroughly professional attitude. It is interesting that during the same period of the English Civil Wars, infantrymen were already accusing gunners of adopting a superior attitude. This, no doubt, was brought on by a growing pride in the science of gunnery, and in the devastating firepower at their fingertips. In an artillery train though, gunners were in the minority. Most of a gun crew were hired labourers, while hired wagoners were used to move the guns around on their carriages. These were civilians, and were there purely to provide the professional gunners with the muscle they needed to operate their guns. This though, was about to change, as during the Age of Reason artillerymen were brought fully into the military fold.

Guns at sea

One of the most dramatic artillery developments of the Renaissance was the introduction of guns at sea. With the exception of those mounted in Mediterranean war galleys guns were a rarity in ships during the 14th and 15th centuries. The basic cog or roundship of the period was tubby and high-sided, and those fitted out as warships usually had fighting platforms (or castles) erected over their bow and stern. These in turn became the forecastle and sterncastle structures used throughout the age of sail. Battles at sea were fought at close quarters, involving volleys of arrows and other missiles such as being aimed at the enemy ship, and then a boarding action, where the two sides fought hand-to-hand. It was only in the mid- to late 14th century that the first guns appeared, although at first these were merely handguns, or larger pieces which were rested on or hooked over the ship's rail. Even the largest of these guns were no bigger than contemporary *ribaudequins*.

Eventually, these increased in size a little, and were mounted onto the ship's gunwale by means of a yoke, a larger version of the rowlock used in modern rowing boats. The guns sat in holes bored in the rail, and the gun could be aimed just like a modern pintle-mounted machine gun. These were given the collective name of 'swivel guns', although a variety of names were used throughout the period, the most common being bases or versos. These could be fired by means of a small powder chamber, and we know from late medieval or 16th-century shipwrecks that spare chambers were often kept close at hand, so the gunners could reload the guns quickly. Essentially these were anti-personnel weapons, designed to be fired at an enemy shortly before the two sides boarded each other. From shipwrecks we also know that these could be loaded with single round shot, or else bags of smaller balls, scrap metal or even nails. This made them deadly close-range weapons.

By the mid-15th century, contemporary illustrations show that larger guns were carried on board ships, usually mounted in the waist, where their weight would cause fewer problems to the ship's stability than if they were in the two castles. These were probably mounted on simple sled carriages, without wheels and, like the smaller swivel guns, were wrought-iron breech-loading guns. Again, from contemporary accounts and from shipwrecks we know these ranged in size, with the larger guns resembling the bombardettas mentioned in the Tower of London inventories. While these could also be loaded with anti-personnel ammunition such as small pieces of scrap metal (called 'lagrange' or 'dice shot'), they could also fire solid ball, which meant that for the first time a ship's guns had the capability to sink other ships using gunfire alone.

By the later 15th century purpose-built royal warships were carrying a large number of guns of various sizes. For instance, in England, Henry VII's *Sovereign*, built in 1485, carried 141

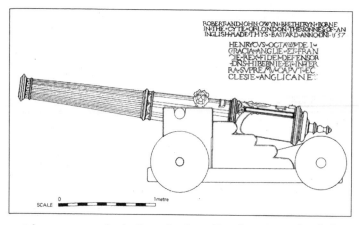

A bronze gun cast by the Owen brothers of London, recovered with the remains of its carriage from the wreck of the Tudor warship Mary Rose, *which sank off Portsmouth in 1546. (Mary Rose Trust)*

guns, of which 110 were described as serpentines or handguns, and the rest were larger stone-shotted guns. Of these, the twenty largest were mounted in her waist, and the rest in her sterncastle. While this shows a move towards the carrying of larger guns at sea, the problem of stability placed a cap on what could safely be carried on board a warship. This changed around 1509, when the first gun ports appeared. It was claimed that these were first invented by a French shipwright, but wherever the idea came from it proved revolutionary. By cutting holes in the hull of a ship, large guns could be mounted closer to the waterline, and so they didn't cause such a danger to the ship's stability.

The same English royal ship, the *Sovereign*, was listed in an inventory of 1509. By then she was only carrying 71 guns – half as many as before – but only 42 of these were listed as serpentines. Instead of the 31 stone-shotted guns she carried in 1495, she was now armed with just 13. However, she now carried ten large bronze guns (described as culverins and curtows), plus six smaller pieces (listed as falcons). This illustrates a new development – the mounting of large bronze guns on board ships. This was clearly the way forward. This development is illustrated by the *Mary Rose*, Henry VIII's great warship. In 1509 she carried 79 guns, of which 33 were serpentines and 26 stone-shotted guns. By 1540 though, after a major refit to strengthen her timbers, she carried 22 large guns, 13 of which were bronze, the rest wrought-iron breech-loaders (described as port-pieces). She also carried 14 smaller guns, and 60 handguns.

When the *Mary Rose* sank in July 1545, she was still carrying this mixed armament of large bronze guns, medium-sized wrought-iron port-pieces and smaller guns, such as swivel guns or handguns. The shipwreck was rediscovered in 1971, and after a decade of excavation her hull was raised in 1982. She is now housed in a purpose-built museum in Portsmouth, and visitors can not only see her varied armament for themselves, but they can also examine all the gun tools, shot and other pieces of equipment needed to operate a 16th-century artillery piece. She remains one of the greatest historical time capsules ever discovered. Her wonders are matched – some would say even exceeded – by the *Vasa*, a large and powerful Swedish royal warship which sank in Stockholm Harbour in 1628.

Together, the two ships illustrate the dramatic changes taking place in ship design during this period. While the *Mary Rose* carried large bronze guns, her mixed armament showed that she was really designed to fight battles at close quarters. By contrast the *Vasa* was a modern sailing ship of war, built primarily to carry her powerful armament of 64 large bronze guns. In this respect she had more in common with Admiral Nelson's flagship HMS *Victory*, which fought at the battle of Trafalgar in 1805, than with the warships of the Tudor age. The Renaissance was a time when gunfounding technology, new shipbuilding techniques and the desire to build floating gun platforms all coalesced to create the heavily armed sailing ship of war.

CHAPTER 3

THE AGE OF REASON

18th century

THE 18TH CENTURY MAY HAVE BEEN regarded as the age of reason and enlightenment, but it was also a time of near-constant warfare in Europe, and an age when the military art developed into a truly scientific endeavour. In artillery, the century was marked by a steady drive towards greater standardisation and perfection, both in terms of the technological development of the guns themselves, as well as in the professionalism of the artillerymen who operated them. This same application of scientific principles would also change the way artillery was used on the battlefield, as some of the great commanders of the age tried to increase the lethal potential of their ordnance. At sea, naval tactics also evolved to make the best possible use of the powerful floating batteries of the age of fighting sail, while new developments in gun design also made their mark, both on land and at sea.

Professionalism

The desire to put artillery on a more professional footing began by bringing gunners into the military fold. Before, while professional gunners operated the artillery pieces, the guns were usually served by civilian labourers, who lacked both the military discipline and the skill or commitment needed to man their guns in the middle of a pitched battle. During the War of the Spanish Succession (1701–14), men were hired when needed, and then the force disbanded when the campaign was over. The exception was the French army, which had a permanent regiment of artillery from 1693. In 1716 the Duke of Marlborough was instrumental in establishing a small permanent force of British artillerymen. While civilian drivers or horses were still hired in time of war, at least the men who crewed the guns were professional artillerymen. At the same time the Austrians took a similar step, while other countries soon followed suit.

This ensured that in the event of a war, a trained and professional body of artillerymen were on hand to take the field. It was increasingly necessary, as the business of serving a gun was gradually becoming more demanding, and gun crews were called upon to follow set-piece drills to ensure greater efficiency, safety and accuracy. Each man had his task and place, and knew how to take over the job of a fellow gun crew member if they fell. While infantrymen were sometimes pressed into service as gunners – usually to manhandle the guns on the battlefield – for the most part the deadly business of gunnery was now left to the professionals. This in turn spawned a growing pride in 'The Art of Gunnery', where a thorough understanding of the scientific principles of ballistics was encouraged in gun captains, along with the empirical knowledge gained from long experience.

Treatises such as Benjamin Robins' *New Principles of Gunnery*, published in 1742, provided the gunners with the scientific knowledge they needed. Robins was an English mathematician who not only applied his skills to ballistics, but also invented tools that gunners could use to put these new-found principles into practice. Thanks to him the ballistic properties of artillery and the trajectory of a ball would be better understood. This allowed scientific tables to be produced, tailored to each type of gun. With these at hand, gunners could more accurately work out what elevation or powder charge to use in order to hit their target. A combination of a growing sense of professionalism among artillerymen and a more scientific approach to gunnery meant that artillery was becoming an increasingly efficient weapon of war.

The standardisation of ordnance

The same scientific precision was also increasingly being applied to the guns themselves. The guns used during the early 18th century were little different from those in use fifty years before. Guns were still cast the same way they had been since the 16th century, and on campaign trains of artillery were notoriously slow, their speed limited by the huge weight of guns, by the lack of suitable horses and limbers, and by the often poor state of roads. So, scientific minds turned their thoughts to increasing the mobility of artillery, and also to producing guns that were both lighter and more reliable. This in turn led to the increasing standardisation of artillery during the century, and to an important change in terminology. Cannons, culverins, demi-culverins and sakers gradually gave way to a classification based on the weight of shot being fired. This would soon become standard practice throughout Europe.

One of the first to embrace this new nomenclature was General John Armstrong, Surveyor General of Britain's artillery. In 1725 he produced a list of regulation sizes for both brass and iron guns, ranging from 42-pounders down to 3-pounders. These not only listed guns by calibre, but by weight and length as well. This meant Armstrong was advocating more than just a change of names. He was proposing the move towards a whole system of artillery, where guns of a certain calibre were all designed alike. In fact Armstrong wasn't the first to come up with this idea. A Dutch treatise of 1645 recommended the designing of a family of guns, 6-, 12-, 24- and 48-pounder weapons, all of the same pattern.

This Dutch idea was embraced by Albert Borgard, a Danish ordnance expert working for the Dutch-born William III of England and I Scotland. He produced drawings of just such a family – or system – of demi-culverins, sakers and minions, which became 9-, 6- and 3-pounder guns respectively. While this system was proposed, there is no evidence it was ever implemented until 1716, when Borgard's complete system was adopted by Britain's Board of Ordnance. His gun plans still survive, as do a few of his 'Borgard system' guns. For the first time, a nation was producing all of its guns to a set pattern.

This guaranteed that guns were being produced to a certain standard, and according to the latest scientific principles. This notion was soon followed by others. In France a similar system was proposed by Florent-Jean de Valliere, an artillery officer who in 1726 became the Director of the Royal Ordnance, Louis XV's equivalent of Britain's Board of Ordnance. Before Valliere, France had adopted a partial system designed by the Swiss-born Jean-Jaques Keller, gunfounder to Louis XIV. However, there were still problems with these late 17th-century guns – they were heavy, and some calibres developed a reputation for bursting when fired. Valliere put an end to that in 1732, when he produced a comprehensive artillery system, covering 4-, 8-, 12-, 16- and 24-pounder guns, as well as mortars.

Calibre	Gun Length (calibres)	Gun Weight (livres*)
4-pounder	25	1,150
8-pounder	24	2,100
12-pounder	23	3,200
16-pounder	22	4,200
24-pounder	20	5,400

* A French *livre* (pound) was the equivalent of 1.1 British pounds.

Valliere's guns weren't just functional – they were real works of art. They were long and slender guns, from 20 to 25 calibres long depending on the shot they fired, with the proportions defined by mathematical formulae and ballistic knowledge to produce what Valliere saw as the perfect gun. Their striking decoration was functional as well as ornamental. Each size of gun had a differently decorated breech – a true gunner could tell the calibre just by glancing at the rear of the gun. The 4-pounder had a face in a sunburst, the emblem of Louis XIV, the 8-pounder sported a monkey's head, the 12-pounder the head of a cock hen, and the 16- and 24-pounder the face of Medusa and Bacchus respectively. The elaborate dolphins – used to lift the gun – looked like they were swimming, while the barrel was decorated with the royal fleur de lys, a scroll carrying the individual name of the gun, and another bearing the Latin inscription *Ultima Ratio Regnum* (The Final Argument of Kings).

The Valliere system was a great step forward, but he only specified the design of the guns themselves. Gun carriages and limbers were still designed by others, and apart from specifying that all of them should be painted red, Valliere paid little heed to their design. He also didn't approve of howitzers, so he never designed a range of barrels for them. Instead the older Keller howitzers were used. The other problem with Valliere's guns was their weight. They weren't really designed to be particularly mobile on the battlefield, and the 4-pounder was too heavy to be easily used as a regimental gun, moving forward in support of the infantry. So, in the 1750s a lighter version was produced, dubbed a Swedish gun in honour of Gustavus Adolphus, the pioneer of regimental guns. These proved a success during the Seven Years War (1756–63), but generally the Valliere guns were outclassed by a new generation of artillery pieces fielded by France's allies and rivals.

In Austria the corresponding artillery system was designed by Artillery General Anton Feuerstein, whose system adopted in 1750 consisted of 3-, 6- and 12-pounder field guns. All of these were just 16 calibres long, while a longer 12-pounder, together

Austrian (Imperialist) mortars and siege guns in action at the siege of Amberg, Bavaria, 1703. (Stratford Archive)

with 18- and 24-pounder guns formed the Austrian siege train. Feuerstein also designed two sizes of howitzer, and four calibres of mortars. Unlike his French counterpart, Feuerstein then designed the gun carriages and limbers to support his guns, thereby creating a fully integrated artillery system, which in the mid-18th century was the envy of Europe.

In neighbouring Prussia artillery systems weren't considered a priority, and the partial system designed by General Christian von Linger in the 1730s was still being used during the Seven Years War. The Linger system consisted of four calibres – 3-, 6-, 12- and 24-pounder guns, the lighter two being designated regimental or field pieces, and the heavier two serving as siege guns. Frederick II 'the Great' approved a new light 3-pounder during the 1740s, while in 1755 a new pattern of 6-pounder was designed by Lieutenant Colonel von Dieskau, which was light enough to be pulled by just four horses. This provided Frederick the Great with the weapon that would form the centrepiece of his one great artillery innovation – the creation of horse artillery.

As a tactical innovator Frederick had wrestled with the problem of providing his cavalry with artillery support. Von Dieskau's gun provided him with a solution. So, during the Seven Years War batteries of horse artillery were formed, the 6-pounders pulled by teams of horses, and ridden by the gunners. This meant the guns could keep up with the cavalry as they advanced. While lightweight 'galloper guns' weren't a new idea, it was Frederick who first applied the idea to a fast-moving horse-drawn battery. However, on the battlefield Frederick made increasing use of his larger guns, particularly the 12-pounders known as 'Brummers', which he reclassified as a field gun and deployed in close support of his infantry. Other commanders before Frederick had used massed gun batteries – for instance the Duke of Marlborough used one at the battle of Ramillies (1709), but it was Frederick who made massed batteries a regular feature on the battlefield.

Other nations also developed their own standardised systems of artillery, and experimented with guns on the battlefield. The Spanish followed the French example and used more ornate guns than the Germanic nations, with ornate lifting dolphins and bulbous multi-ringed muzzles. These guns were more squat than their French counterparts, the product of the early 18th-century designs of the Del Voye y Habet family of gunfounders, who served the Spanish crown. The Spanish intent was to have guns that served equally well in fortresses, at sea or in the field. However, the Spanish only used cast-iron guns at sea or as garrison pieces. Later 18th-century Spanish artillery were almost direct copies of the new French Gribeauval system. This French influence was understandable – both countries were ruled by the House of Bourbon, which led to close political, economic and military ties between the two kingdoms.

Another prominent gunfounding nation was Sweden. Their ordnance industry supplied naval guns to most of Europe, both for use in royal warships and in merchant vessels. Most of these were cast-iron pieces, and from the mid-17th century the squat cast-iron gun known as a 'Finnbanker' proved particularly popular due to its compact size compared to its bore, its reliability, and its affordability. Similar guns were produced in Denmark, although these appear to have been exclusively for Danish use. The fledgling United States of America produced guns of its own after 1775, as well as using French or British pieces, but for the most part their own designs followed British patterns. In America a standardised national train of artillery wasn't developed until the early 19th century, shortly before the Anglo-American conflict known as the War of 1812.

The Blomfield system

In Britain the system devised by General John Armstrong served the country well during the Seven Years War, and the American War of Independence. By then though, the system was generally seen as being outdated. Back in 1742 a treatise called *New Principles of Gunnery* had been published, written by the English-born mathematician Benjamin Robins. His work represented a new step forward in the understanding of ballistics. While some of his ideas, such as the use of rifled guns firing elongated projectiles, were too far ahead of their time to be taken seriously, his study of the effectiveness of artillery of different calibres demonstrated that larger guns were proportionately more deadly than smaller pieces. This view was shared by the German-born mathematician John Muller, whose *Treatise of Artillery* was published in 1757. In it he supported Robins' claims, and added that existing British guns were needlessly long and heavy. This meant the guns of the Armstrong system, as well as the older pieces designed by Albert Borgard, many of which were still in service.

While this criticism may have been valid, at least Muller called Armstrong's system 'the least deficient' of those in use in

Europe at the time. Muller was influential – he was the head of the Royal Military Academy in Woolwich – and due to his influence the guns of the Armstrong system were reduced in length, from barrels which were 20–25 calibres long down to ones of 15 calibres (or 16 calibres for naval guns). Muller actually preferred even shorter barrels, but this was as far as the British Board of Ordnance were willing to go. Bronze guns were still longer than cast-iron ones. For instance, in Muller's treatise he records that old-fashioned (Armstrong or Borgard pattern) bronze 12-pounders were 9 feet long, while his own versions measured 6 feet 7 inches. Cast-iron guns of the same calibre were 5 feet in length, or 5 feet 6 inches for guns used at sea. The general trend though, was for shorter and lighter guns.

A new partial system was developed by General Thomas Desagulier in 1775, with covered 1-, 3-, 6- and 12-pounder bronze guns. Contrary to Muller's principles these were longer than normal British field guns of the time, but in action they proved to be more accurate than their shorter counterparts. The 12-pounder though, was found to be too heavy and was discontinued, although the smaller calibres remained in use during the first decades of the 19th century. These Desagulier pieces were designed empirically, rather than through the application of strict mathematical principles. A far more scientific and complete system followed ten years later, in 1785. Designed by Thomas Blomfield, the Inspector of Artillery, this new system drew on all the latest scientific knowledge, as well as advances in gunfounding and Blomfield's own practical knowledge, based on two decades of experience.

Blomfield was an interesting character. The son of a clergyman, he joined the Royal Navy, and took part in the British naval victory over the French at Quiberon Bay in 1759 before transferring to the army. As a young artillery officer he saw service in the Americas, and in 1777 he was wounded while fighting the Americans at Saratoga. He served as the aid to the Master General of the Ordnance, and then in 1780 he was named as the new Inspector of Artillery at Woolwich. He was responsible for proofing all new guns, and he courted controversy when he rejected almost 500 of them during his first year in the post. This though, forced an improvement in gunfounding standards, which had become slipshod. He then turned his mind to the redesign of artillery, and after conducting numerous experiments he produced his own system, which was approved in 1785.

His emphasis on standardisation led to the manufacture of simple but elegant guns, shorter than those of earlier systems, but reliable and practical pieces, designed to be functional both as naval guns and as field pieces. Although he designed both bronze and cast-iron guns, and mortars and howitzers, his main success came with his designs for 6-pounder and 9-pounder guns – weapons that would form the backbone of Britain's field artillery for a quarter of a century. There was no superfluous decoration – these were practical guns for a new industrial age. As well as proving excellent field pieces, especially when mounted on Blomfield's own design of carriages, these guns were also meant to be as easy to cast as possible. This in turn encouraged the rapid production of artillery, just a decade before Britain became embroiled in a new global war against France and her allies.

In fact, the mass production of reliable artillery pieces had been made that much easier thanks to the invention of the Swiss engineer Johan Maritz (1680–1743). In 1712 he travelled to France, and tried to persuade both gunfounders and the staff of the Royal Ordnance that his invention would revolutionise gun production. He argued that if a barrel was cast as a solid piece and then bored out, then the size of the internal bore would be far more precise. This meant the gun would be more accurate. Maritz designed a vertical hydraulically powered boring machine that could do the job with precision. His first designs were imperfect, and it wasn't until 1734 that he finally perfected his design, this time as a machine which worked horizontally rather than vertically.

Gunfounders preparing the mould of an artillery piece in the royal gun foundry at Woolwich, mid-18th century. (Stratford Archive)

He finally managed to convince Jean-Florent de Valliere of the merits of his machine, which proved its worth in the royal foundry in Strasbourg. Effectively the boring machine functioned a little like a modern industrial lathe, and could bore a gun out in less than three days. Before Maritz' death in 1743 Valliere approved the adoption of the boring machine, which became a standard piece of apparatus in French gun foundries. All of the guns designed by Valliere were produced using this method.

Industrial espionage was no new phenomenon, and soon word of this breakthrough reached foreign ears, first in Austria, then Prussia and then in Britain. By the end of the Seven Years War in 1763 the boring machine was in general use throughout Europe, although Britain's royal foundry in Woolwich only adopted it in the early 1770s. By then though, the Industrial Revolution was gathering pace. Recent improvements in the way iron was mined and smelted led to a dramatic increase in iron production, first in Britain and then elsewhere in Europe. Machinery like Maritz' boring machine could now be operated by hydraulic power, while steam power was gradually being developed, and would eventually replace it. One by-product of this new industrial age was the relative ease with which high-quality artillery could be produced, compared to just a few decades before. The result was a new generation of well-designed and perfectly cast guns, ready to take the field.

Specialised ordnance

While the majority of these 18th-century artillery pieces were conventional guns, with a barrel length at least 15 times the width of the bore, there were several other groups of guns which didn't fit the conventional mould. The oldest of these ordnance types was the mortar, which effectively looked like one of those *pot de fer* weapons of the 14th century. This was because it had a large bore and a small barrel length – more like a large and heavily reinforced powder chamber. Unlike regular guns, which fired their shot directly at a target, these were indirect fire weapons. This meant they threw their projectile up into the air at a high angle, and if the gunner calculated his shot correctly it would then plunge down onto the target, as if falling out of the sky.

The real advantage of a mortar was its ability to fire over the top of enemy defences. This really made it a siege weapon, and traditionally mortars were attached to the siege train. Unlike other guns a mortar had no carriage – instead its trunnions which were sited at the end of the cascabel rather than halfway along the barrel. These sat in a slot in a wooden base or block. This description of a mortar written in 1705 summed up this weapon admirably: 'A mortar piece is a sort of short piece of artillery, reinforced, and of a wide calibre, differing from a cannon in both form and use. The cannon serves to throw a ball, and the mortar to throw bombs, carcasses, firepots and several other sorts of fireworks.' This wasn't strictly true – mortars could fire solid stone or cast-iron round shot, but their real value lay in lobbing explosive bombs over the walls of a town or fortress.

These bombs were like over-sized contemporary *grenadoes* (grenades) – a fuse was ignited when the mortar was fired, and the bomb would explode when the fuse reached the powder charge inside it, shattering the bomb casing and scattering shards of metal all around it. The carcass mentioned above was a small oval-shaped cage which contained incendiary materials, and was designed to set houses on fire. The firepot was a similar type of incendiary, usually made from thick clay, but like the grenadoe which succeeded it this was a hand-thrown projectile. The description of 1705 used this older term to mean a hollow metal sphere fitted with a fuse – in other words a bomb. During this period mortars came in a range of sizes. The same description of 1705 declared; 'The land mortars most used in England are 10, 13, 15 and 18 inches diameter. There are [also] smaller mortars of 6 and 8 inches.'

These small mortars existed before this, but in the early 18th century the Dutch engineer Baron Menno van Coehorn (or Cohorn) invented a small 4-inch diameter mortar, less than a foot long, and with a fixed elevation of 45 degrees. Normally grenadoes were thrown by hand, but Coehorn's mortars were effectively grenade throwers, with a set range of about 200 yards. Van Coehorn was a fortifications expert – the Dutch answer to Vauban – and he recognised the need for large numbers of these little grenade throwers to protect his siege trenches from attack. Regular mortars though, had a range of between 2,000 and 4,000 yards, depending on their calibre and elevation, and so had a range equivalent to or greater than the largest siege guns of their day. As indirect fire weapons they also had a minimum range of around 400–500 yards, unlike conventional guns which could still fire at an enemy at point-blank range.

While the howitzer had first been developed in the 16th century, it was during this period that it evolved into a practical weapon. The howitzer combined the qualities of the mortar and the conventional gun. The same list of gun descriptions from 1705 gives these the delightful name of 'Hobits'. The entry ran; 'Hobits are sort of small mortars, about 8 inches diameter, some 7, some 6. They differ nothing from a mortar but in their carriage, which is made after the fashion of a gun carriage, only much shorter.' A more detailed definition from 1779 claimed that 'A howitz is a kind of mortar, mounted on a field carriage like a gun. The difference between a mortar and a howitz is that the trunnions of the first are at the end, and in the middle in the last.' Eventually the term 'howitzer' was adopted, from the German *haubitze*, itself derived from *houfen*, meaning a crowd of people. This suggests the gun was originally designed as an anti-personnel weapon.

As early as the mid-17th century, gunners experimented with the mounting of mortars on regular gun carriages, but these proved ineffective. However, in 1686–87 a Tower of London inventory lists a '10-inch hawbitz', while inventories from 1713 list a range of differently sized 'howitz' pieces. The advantage of a 'howitz' or 'howitzer' over a mortar was that it could be fired at any distance from the target, out to its maximum range and elevation, and was capable of both direct and indirect fire. They were also lighter than mortars of the same calibre, as they tended to be less strongly reinforced, and being mounted on gun carriages they were also more mobile. This made the howitzer a versatile weapon, capable of operating like a mortar when required, but essentially its ability to fire anti-personnel projectiles was what guaranteed its place in the 18th-century military arsenal.

The howitzer was an 18th-century success story, which is more than could be said about other unusual pieces of ordnance. In 1724 one French soldier, Jean Charles, the Chevalier Folard, advocated the abandonment of gunpowder weapons, and a return to more reliable catapults and other torsion engines. He also recommended the abandonment of muskets in favour of longbows. Fortunately for the French army his suggestions were ignored. A far more capable French military innovator was Maurice de Saxe, the leading French general of the mid-18th century. His answer to the lack of mobility of the French artillery train was the *amusette*, an over-sized musket which fired a ½-pound ball, and which would be deployed in large numbers in support of the infantry.

This idea was also developed by another French military thinker, the Marquis de Bonneville, who in 1762 advocated the adoption of a similar weapon. While the *amusette* was little more than a large musket, de Boneville's invention was a 1-pounder breech-loading gun, mounted on a small carriage or cart. Despite the survival of a few speculative engravings, there is no evidence guns of this type ever took to the field. Essentially, in their quest for artillery mobility, both of these French innovators had re-invented the medieval *ribaudequin*. While their ideas failed to catch on, *amusettes* were adopted on an experimental basis by several European armies of the time. Consequently they were used in small numbers throughout the rest of the century, particularly in North America, where the wooded or rugged terrain often prevented the deployment of larger and more conventional artillery pieces.

A more effective solution to the problem of battlefield mobility was the 'galloper gun'. During the 1720s the Austrians mounted lightweight versions of their 4-pounder and 8-pounder guns on specially adapted carriages with two limber poles, designed to be fitted on either side of a horse team, arrayed one horse behind another. The idea was that these gun teams could gallop into action, and then the weapons could be fired without the guns being unlimbered. While this proved impractical due to the practicalities of both horse handling and the operation of the gun itself, the basic idea was not without merit, as it encouraged the use of highly mobile light field guns. These first made an appearance in the 1740s, and were found to be effective once the two-poled carriage was actually unlimbered. They also proved the fore-runner of the 6-pounder horse artillery guns pioneered by Frederick the Great.

Artillery on the battlefield

The age of reason could just as easily be called the century of warfare. War seemed to rage almost continually in one part of Europe after another, while the rival crowns of Britain, France and Spain extended this conflict to the high seas, or to other continents. Then came the American War of Independence (1775–83), in which the Americans were supported by Britain's European adversaries as they tried to profit from the rebellion. What all this fighting did do though, was to give gunners an opportunity to perfect their science, and for generals to learn how to get the best from their increasingly powerful train of artillery.

The Great Northern War (1700–21) involving Sweden, Russia, Poland and Denmark saw the Russian army of Tsar Peter the Great evolve into a potent fighting force. Until 1709 Charles XII and his Swedes were all-victorious in the conflict. This ended with Tsar Peter's great victory on the battlefield of Poltava, a battle won largely through the decisive firepower of Russian artillery. While Peter's artillery arm was becoming increasingly professional, it was still a force wedded to the tactics of the preceding century. By contrast, during the War of the Spanish Succession the Duke of Marlborough developed new ways to deploy his artillery on the battlefield. Again, until his string of Allied victories over the French in Germany and Flanders the French artillery train was regarded as the best in Europe. By forming large massed batteries, and concentrating fire where it was needed most, Marlborough managed to outshoot the French, and so help secure his string of Allied victories.

The French army remained a formidable force though, and during the War of the Austrian Succession (1740–48) it won a major victory over its opponents at the battle of Fontenoy (1745), thanks to the generalship of Marshal de Saxe – the advocate of the *amusette*. Before the campaign began, de Saxe reorganised his army into ad-hoc divisions of around 6,000–10,000 infantry each, and then divided up his train of artillery, so that each division had its own dedicated artillery support. This proved so successful that the arrangement was eventually adopted by almost all European armies.

The Seven Years War was another conflict that involved most of Europe's military powers, although the conflict came to be dominated by the military activities of Prussia's Frederick the Great. It was he who first developed a functional horse artillery arm, to operate in direct support of his cavalry, but he also advocated the use of regimental guns, and the forming of grand batteries. His main opponents were Austria and Russia, both of which had powerful artillery arms of their own. The Russians in particular pioneered their own form of howitzer called a 'licorne', which proved highly successful. Less so was Shuvalov's 'secret howitzer', a smaller weapon with an elliptical bore designed to provide close-range fire support to the Russian infantry.

In the west, Britain and her German allies fought the French in a string of hard-fought battles which were essentially repeats of the previous wars between the same two sides. Less conventional though, were the campaigns fought overseas, in the Caribbean, North America and in India. In most of these campaigns artillery played a relatively modest part due to the terrain, which didn't usually lend itself to the transport of heavy guns. This wasn't a problem in India though, and while the British and their Indian allies had a relatively small artillery train, the French enjoyed the support of an Indian ally who owned the largest artillery train in the sub-continent.

At the battle of Plassey in 1757 the British guns outshot their Indian counterparts, thanks to their improved mobility, rate of fire and the better training of their gun crews. Just as importantly, the powder of the Indian guns was soaked during a pre-battle storm, while the British kept their powder dry. Incidentally, the handful of French guns present at the battle were handled well, and the actions of their gunners were later praised by the battle's victor, Colonel Clive, later known as 'Clive of India'. In the Americas, guns were mainly used as siege weapons, and were used with good effect by both sides. However, the problems encountered in transporting guns through the American wilderness led both the French and the British to adopt light galloper guns, which were better suited to the geography of North America.

These guns certainly proved their worth in the next conflict fought there – the American War of Independence. At first the Americans relied on captured British guns, but soon began casting ordnance of their own, based largely on contemporary British patterns. This influence was encouraged by the publication of a copy of John Muller's *A Treatise of Artillery* in Philadelphia, but these early American guns were often crude affairs compared to the supremely professional output of British gunfounders. From 1777 on the Americans also enjoyed extensive French support, and in a number of engagements including the siege of Yorktown, the presence of French artillery had a decisive impact on the course of the campaign, and probably the war.

All this martial experience helped force European (and now also American) artillery into a powerful and homogenous force, with guns in a variety of calibres cast using the latest techniques, and mounted on robust modern field carriages, or on garrison carriages lining the walls of fortifications. The development and use of artillery at sea during 'The Age of Fighting Sail' will be covered in the next chapter, when guns dramatically influenced both ship design and tactics. On land, artillery might have begun the century as a relatively minor military arm, but by its end it had become a crucial element in the military toolkit. What artillery really needed now – to raise it to the position of being the arbiter of victory on the battlefield – was an inspirational military commander who knew exactly how to make the most of his guns.

CHAPTER 4

THE WARS OF NAPOLEON

1792–1815

WHILE MOST OF THE CHAPTERS IN this book cover broad historical periods, this is one of three that highlights one particular conflict or era. While this chapter focuses on the Napoleonic Wars (1803–15), it also embraces the decade-long French Revolutionary War (1792–1802). The result is a snapshot of the state of European artillery in this key era. It was a time when the smooth-bore muzzle-loading gun had reached the pinnacle of its technological evolution. While these guns would remain in service until the second half of the 19th century, these later guns were little different from the ones which fought on Napoleonic-era battlefields from New Orleans to Cairo, and Moscow to Cape Town.

Napoleon

During this period, the main protagonists were France, Austria, Britain, Prussia, Russia and Spain. Other smaller military powers sided with either France or the Allies or, like some of the larger ones, occasionally changed their allegiance according to political necessity. The war would also embrace the archaic forces of the

Ottoman Empire, the fledgling army of the United States of America, and the defenders of Spain's sprawling overseas empire. It would be fought at sea as well as on land. It also was the apogee of the Age of Fighting Sail, when the largest ships-of-the-line were essentially floating batteries of immense destructive power. These warships would fight in a string of sea fights, the most famous of which was the battle of Trafalgar (1805), when French and Spanish naval power was decisively broken, thanks to the superiority of British naval gunnery. Above all though, it was the era of Napoleon Bonaparte, a man who understood the power of the gun.

As a Corsican, Napoleon Bonaparte (1769–1821) was an outsider in metropolitan France, but in France's military colleges he overcame the taint of provincialism by excelling at his studies. In 1784 he was commissioned into the artillery, but when the French Revolution erupted five years later he returned to Corsica to promote the revolution on the island. In 1793 he was recalled to take charge of the gun batteries besieging the royalist stronghold of Toulon. His eye for terrain identified the weak point in the port's defences, and after capturing it his guns were able to force the evacuation of the Allied fleet, and the surrender of the town. His use of artillery on the streets of Paris to suppress a counter-revolutionary rising displayed a ruthless streak that earned him the command of the Army of Italy. That marked the start of his rise to power.

Bonaparte's whirlwind campaign against the Austrians in Italy in 1795–96 clearly demonstrated his outstanding ability as a military commander. Less successful was his subsequent expedition to Egypt, which ended in failure, but only after Bonaparte had abandoned his stranded army and returned home to further his political career. His political manoeuvrings secured his position as one of France's ruling triumvirate, and after further victories in Italy in 1800 he became the First Consul – effectively France's sole ruler. This title wasn't enough though, and in 1804 he became the self-proclaimed Emperor Napoleon I. Most of Europe saw him

A French Guard horse artillery piece in action in a detail from The
Battle of Waterloo, *a painting by William Allen.(Stratford Archive)*

as an upstart, and a fresh anti-French coalition was formed to
oppose him. Bonaparte – now just Napoleon – dealt with this
by winning a string of great victories, at Austerlitz (1805), Jena-
Auerstadt (1806), Friedland (1807) and Wagram (1809). By then
most of Europe lay at his feet, and Napoleon's power had reached
its zenith.

After that, a string of miscalculations led to the gradual
unravelling of his empire. His invasion of Spain in 1807 was a huge
miscalculation. The guerrilla war that followed sapped his military
strength while a string of victories by the Anglo-Portuguese army
in Spain eroded the will of the commanders Napoleon left in Spain
to fight the war there. An even greater blunder was his invasion
of Russia in 1812. That summer his 'Grand Army' appeared
unstoppable, but the Russian 'scorched earth' policy, a gruelling
stalemate of a battle at Borodino, the burning of Moscow and the
onset of winter all contributed to the army's destruction. After
that Napoleon was on the defensive, and for all his military genius
his army was eventually bundled out of Germany in 1813, and
forced back into France. There, a brilliant but doomed last-ditch
campaign to save the empire ended in failure when the Allies
captured Paris, and Napoleon was forced to abdicate.

His comfortable exile on Elba didn't last long. The following summer he returned, reclaimed France, and so initiated the Hundred Days Campaign, which ended in a final defeat at the battle of Waterloo (1815). This time his exile was permanent, and he died on remote St. Helena six years later. This bald, brief outline of Napoleon Bonaparte's career barely scratches the surface of his influence on Europe during his lifetime. He transformed the French army from a rabble infused with revolutionary fervour into a fighting machine that was the envy of Europe. Throughout his military career his achievements were underpinned by his expert use of artillery. As a gunner he knew how to make the most of his ordnance, and when he once said that 'It is with guns that war is made', he knew what he was talking about. Strangely, for one so steeped in the use of artillery, he never really understood naval warfare, where naval gunnery was the real arbiter of victory at sea.

Napoleonic artillery

Across Europe each of the major states and many of the minor ones had their own patterns of artillery. Some were heavily influenced by the artillery systems of other countries, but for the most part there was no standardisation. Each nation simply followed their own path. Another factor that made standardisation difficult was the variety of weights and measures which existed throughout Europe at the time. For instance, 100 pounds in Britain weighed the same as 82 pounds in Geneva, 90 in Frankfurt, 92 in Paris and Amsterdam, 97 in Antwerp, 104 in Lisbon, 113 in Moscow, 137 in Genoa, and 152 in Venice. So, a 6-pounder gun in one country didn't necessarily fire the same size of ball as a 6-pounder in another part of Europe. Still, almost all of these artillery pieces conformed to the two main groups – conventional long guns and short-barrelled howitzers.

Austrian artillery of the Napoleonic Wars, watercolour, c. 1809.
(Stratford Archive)

Most European armies of the late 18th century were equipped with a mixture of 3-pounder, 6-pounder and 12-pounder field guns, as well as howitzers. The larger military powers also maintained a siege train of larger guns. Artillery pieces of various sizes were also used in coastal defence batteries, and in the defence of fortresses. The exceptions when it came to field guns were France, Spain and Bavaria, all of which followed the French practice of using 4-pounder, 8-pounder and 12-pounder field guns. The size of howitzers varied more widely – Austria, Prussia and Russia used 7-pounder and 10-pounder weapons, while the French and the British classified theirs by bore size – 4.4-inch and 5.5-inch for the British, and 6-inch and 8-inch howitzers for the French. This profusion of calibres though, was secondary to the understanding that across Europe, guns were largely used in the same way, regardless of the small regional differences.

The popularity of the 3-, 6- and 12-pounder group of guns was largely due to the influence of Austria, who introduced these calibres into their artillery system before the Seven Years War. At the time they were widely regarded as having the most advanced ordnance in Europe, and so inevitably other countries followed their lead. This included Prussia, Austria's main rival during the Seven Years War. The difference was, while the Austrians favoured their lighter guns on the battlefield, Frederick the Great of Prussia put his faith in light regimental guns, and in his powerful 12-pounders. His battlefield successes led to the adoption of lighter 3-pounders in other European armies, and the greater use of 12-pounders. Similarly his employment of light 6-pounder galloper guns as horse artillery pieces was copied elsewhere, together with light howitzers. Effectively, during the later 18th century Prussia took over the Austrian mantle as the continent's leading artillery power.

Across Europe, 12-pounders remained the heaviest guns used as field pieces, and 18-pounders, 24-pounders and even huge 32-pounders were restricted to the siege train, or were used as 'garrison artillery' deployed in static defences. All but fortress guns used similar gun carriages – the guns sitting between two trails, the whole carriage sitting on two large spoked wheels. The British were the exception, and during this period their field guns were mounted on block-trail carriages, with a single central trail rather than two. The way guns were organised into batteries varied slightly from country to country, but essentially these all followed a similar pattern, with four to twelve guns operating as a single unit on the battlefield, supported by their attendant limbers, ammunition caissons, field forges and storage wagons.

The French though, were the leading proponents of a completely integrated artillery that embraced all this rolling stock, as well as the guns and carriages themselves. As a result it was the French whose artillery would prove the most influential during this period, at least in terms of others copying French innovations and artillery organisation.

The Gribeauval system

In the early 18th century the Valliere system was the first of its kind in Europe, and rightly established the French as the leading artillery designers of the age. These guns were both beautiful and reliable, but this came at a price. They were extremely heavy, and by the mid-18th century other countries, such as Austria and Britain, were producing lighter and less heavily decorated guns that were every bit as good. This made them more mobile than the French ordnance. During the Seven Years War France and Austria were allies, and a French artillery officer called Jean-Baptiste de Gribeauval was seconded to the Austrian army. He considered the Austrian guns superior to those in French service, and on his return to Paris after the war he said as much. By that time he was an influential figure in artillery circles, having been rewarded by the Austrians for his help in designing new kinds of fortress guns and explosive ammunition. He was now ready to make his mark back home.

Gribeauval was now a major general, and in 1756 he was appointed the new Inspector of Artillery. Now he was in a position to introduce the reforms he felt were so badly needed. He began by devolving the task of crewing naval guns to the fleet, and reorganised the remaining body of gunners into battalions (later regiments) and companies. Each company supplied the manpower for an artillery battery. Next came the development of a new system of artillery – bitterly opposed by many senior figures in the army, and by de Valliere's son Joseph, who didn't want to see his father's legacy rendered obsolete. However, the new system was duly approved by Louis XVI in October 1765. The Gribeauval system would now supplant the Valliere one.

This system was the first to offer a unified design for everything from gun carriages, carriages and limbers down to individual gun tools. Gribeauval began by dividing artillery into four categories – field guns, siege guns, garrison guns and

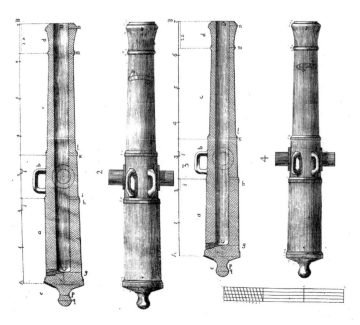

Gun barrels of the Gribeauval system, first introduced into French service in 1765. (Stratford Archive)

coastal guns. All guns larger than 12-pounders were relegated to the last three categories, making the 12-pounder the largest field gun in French service. Like Valliere, Gribeauval based his system around 4-, 8- and 12-pounder pieces, as well as the 6-inch howitzer. These new guns had a much smaller windage than their predecessors (the gap between the calibre of the barrel and the diameter of the shot). This reduced the amount of powder needed, which allowed the walls of the gun to be thinner. He also shortened the length of the barrels, which in turn meant that gun carriages could he shorter and lighter too.

As a result at 1,936 pounds (880 kg), Gribeauval's 12-pounder barrel was half the weight of the Valliere one, and at 7½ feet long and 17 calibres it was two thirds of the length. It could fire a ball just as far though, and with the same degree of accuracy.

This was the most successful of his field guns, and the design remained unaltered throughout the Napoleonic Wars. However, during the French Revolutionary War both the 4-pounder and the 8-pounder were deemed too heavy by gunners in the field, even though they were both considerably lighter than their Valliere equivalent. It seemed that he hadn't taken into account the great speed with which French Revolutionary armies could move on campaign, compared to the professionally trained forces opposing them. As Gribeauval died in 1789, in the same month as the French Revolution began, it was left to others to improve on his designs.

While the plain, largely unadorned brass Gribeauval gun and howitzer barrels were effective, they were only part of the Gribeauval system. It also covered gun carriages, all designed to a standard pattern. Where possible, the same carriage was used for guns of different calibres, to make it easier to replace damaged carriages in the field. This meant that the 8-pounder and the 12-pounder shared the same carriage, as did the 4-pounder and the 6-inch howitzer. Interestingly, the carriage for these larger guns had two slots for the trunnions – one to be used when the gun was limbered, and the other when it was unlimbered, and made ready to fire. While this increased the time spent preparing the guns for action, it greatly improved the weight distribution of the gun when it was being towed by its limber and horse team.

Gribeauval also designed caissons to carry extra ammunition, field forges to repair the guns and carriages in the field, and even ammunition wagons to carry spare powder or tools. This mean that when Napoleon's army went on campaign it was supported by a fully comprehensive artillery system, with all the equipment it needed to make its mark on the battlefield. Gribeauval also turned his attention to siege guns and carriages, and those used in fortresses or coastal batteries. Garrison and coastal artillery pieces of his design came in four sizes – 8-, 12-, 16- and 24-pounders, as well as 10- and 12-inch mortars. The two largest gun sizes were also used as siege guns, while enormous naval 36-pounder guns were also used in coastal batteries. While the siege carriages resembled other land carriages, the larger guns in forts and coastal batteries were mounted on carriages designed to recoil along a sloping wooden ramp, the incline absorbing the gun's recoil.

Finally, Gribeauval's reforms extended to education. All French gunners now went through an extensive programme of training, which progressively taught recruits their trade, and then went on to improve their professional knowledge through further training. While this was done to some extent by all European countries of the period, Gribeauval was the first to integrate this with regional training centres, based in the main French artillery depots, and to institute regular drills and inspections, to help the men retain their skills. After Gribeauval died his work was continued by his former pupils, including Jean du Beaumont, Baron du Teil, whose working association with Napoleon helped encourage the future Emperor's professional skills as an artillery officer.

During the French Revolutionary War the French captured a large number of enemy guns, particularly 6-pounder pieces in Austrian, Prussian or Russian service. This windfall coincided with the rise of complaints from serving artillery officers that the Gribeauval 8-pounder was too heavy to be deployed easily in the field. The solution was to press these lighter captured 6-pounders into French service, mount them on Gribeauval-style carriages, and then to gradually phase out the heavier 8-pounders. Before this could be done though, all of the pieces had to be re-bored to conform to the French poundage system. These guns were designated the Year XI system 6-pounder, a partial system introduced in 1803 (year 11 of the revolution). They proved successful, although the older 8-pounders remained in service for several years.

By this time Napoleon had decided to abandon the 4-pounder, as he regarded regimental guns as more of an encumbrance than a tactical advantage. Some of these were re-bored as 6-pounders, but the bulk were placed in store. The 6-pounder therefore became the lowest-calibre gun in the army, at least for a while. After 1809, Napoleon noted that the quality of his infantry were declining. So he re-introduced 4-pounder regimental guns, to bolster his infantry's defensive firepower. However, this time they were provided when needed, rather than forming a permanent attachment to every infantry formation. So, despite these changes the Gribeauval system remained in use from before the French Revolution until the end of the Napoleonic Wars. It was these Gribeauval guns that Napoleon used throughout Europe, and which played such a crucial part in his military endeavours.

Napoleon's rivals

When Britain and Revolutionary France declared war in 1793 the British army was equipped with 3-, 6- and 9-pounder field guns. The Royal Artillery regarded the cumbersome 12-pounder as a siege gun, therefore it sat alongside the 18- and 24-pounder guns in the siege train. These larger guns were also used in field fortifications and coastal batteries, together with enormous 32- and 48-pounder cast-iron pieces and an array of mortars. The British also used a 5½-inch howitzer in the field, while larger howitzers formed part of the siege train. The 3-pounder was a regimental (or battalion) gun, and so they stood apart from the army's main artillery formations, which therefore used 6-pounders and 9-pounders in the field.

A particular British innovation was the block carriage. Most other European guns used conventional carriages, with the gun resting on transoms between the two long checks. This was how most guns had been mounted since the 16th century, despite experiments with other methods. In the 1790s though, the British introduced the block carriage which just had one wide cheek, like a single tail. This allowed the gun to be turned (or trained) more easily, and it was also lighter. It was first introduced to serve British 6-pounder horse-artillery guns, but once its virtues were seen the block carriage was used elsewhere, first in howitzers and then for all field guns. Larger guns, of 12-pounder calibre and above, retained the conventional two-cheeked carriage.

Austria and Prussia also used guns of the same variety of calibres as the British, although for them the 12-pounder remained an acceptable field piece, and was used to form an artillery reserve. Both of these countries produced their own guns, conforming to their own artillery systems. However, these were now outdated, having first been introduced in the mid-18th century. The loss of much of their artillery in the campaigns of 1805–07 led to a re-evaluation. This in turn led to the virtual imitation of the Gribeauval design, albeit only for 6-pounder and 12-pounder guns. Where possible the old 3-pounder regimental guns were replaced in the field by light 6-pounders operating in close-support batteries, while other light 6-pounders were used by batteries of horse artillery. Similarly, while in 1793 the Austrians used 3-, 7- and 10-pounder howitzers, the larger and smaller pieces were eventually replaced by improved 7-pounder howitzers.

This said, the Prussians still retained a few 3-pounders, grouped in batteries, but for the most part the 6-pounder was their preferred field gun, supported by batteries of 12-pounders which formed a corps or army reserve. In Spain, while the rest of the army was of dubious military value, the artillery was reliable and effective. As Spain and pre-revolutionary France were both ruled by the house of Bourbon, military co-operation between the two countries was encouraged, and so in the late 18th century the Spanish adopted the Gribeauval system, albeit using guns cast in Spain.

Russia often adopted military developments from elsewhere in Europe, but for the most part it forged its own military path. During the Seven Years War the Russians developed an excellent artillery system of their own, and these Shuvalov system guns were still in service in 1793. These 3-, 6-, 8- and 12-pounder guns and 9- and 12-pounder licornes (howitzers) were augmented by the usual range of larger siege guns and mortars. After the disastrous Austerlitz campaign of 1805 a reform was instituted by General

Alexei Arakeef, the Inspector of Artillery. His 1805 system reduced the range of calibres to just 6-pounder and 12-pounder guns, and 3-, 10- and 20-pounder licornes. The smallest licorne proved ineffective, and was withdrawn in 1810, but the remaining four guns and howitzers formed the backbone of Russia's artillery arm during the Napoleonic Wars.

Projectiles

As it had been for centuries, during the Napoleonic era the cast-iron spherical round shot remained the most commonly used artillery projectile. Obviously the weight of these balls corresponded to the weight of the gun firing them, so a 12-pounder fired a 12-pound ball. However, there were minor variations, and the calibre of the gun itself was always fractionally wider than the diameter of the shot, to prevent it jamming inside the barrel. This gap (the windage) varied slightly from one gun type to another, but generally the tendency was to keep this windage as small as possible, to prevent the explosive force of the ignited gunpowder from leaking out around the sides of the ball as it was blasted out of the barrel. The ball, after all, was an inert lump of metal. What turned it into a deadly projectile was the tremendous force and movement imparted to it by the gunpowder.

The range of a gun depended on factors such as elevation, gun size and the amount of powder used, but in general the larger the gun, the greater its range and velocity. A French 4-pounder had an effective range of around 750 yards, compared to 900 yards for a French 12-pounder. This though, was when the gun was fired directly at a target. If the gun was elevated slightly then these ranges increased to 1,200 and 1,800 yards respectively. At these longer ranges the ball followed a more elliptical flight path, and so hit the target at a slight angle, like an arrow falling from the sky, rather than head-on. When a ball landed it tended to bounce a few times, following the same line of flight. On the battlefield this meant that it could strike the target, then continue wreaking havoc among troops further behind it.

Traditionally, the powder charge weighed about a third of the weight of the projectile. It was inserted first, followed by the ball, and then by a wad to hold it in place. By the late 18th century it was common for the iron round shot and the disc-shaped wooden wad to be combined into a sabot round, the two parts bound together by thin iron straps. This greatly speeded the business of loading. So, a cylindrical cloth powder bag was inserted into the barrel, followed by the sabot. This though was superseded shortly after 1800 when fixed ammunition was developed. Here the powder charge and the sabot were all bound together into one unit, usually by nailing the charge bag to the underside of the sabot. While fixed (or ready) ammunition was originally designed for situations where rapid fire was needed, most gunners preferred this type of ammunition, and used it throughout a battle. This was the forerunner of the modern artillery shell – a single container combining both the propellant and the projectile.

When the enemy approached within a few hundred yards of the gun the crew would switch to firing canister. It could be fired

A Gribeauval 4-pounder gun in action at the Battle of the Pyramids (1798), in a detail of a painting by Louis Lejeune. (Stratford Archive)

by both guns and howitzers, and usually consisted of a sealed cylindrical tin with a diameter a little less than the calibre of the gun, and with a wooden sabot attached to the base of it. Inside the tin were dozens of musket balls packed in sawdust. When the gun was fired the tin disintegrated, and the musket balls fanned out in a deadly cone. Canister range was around 400 yards for a 4-pounder, and almost 600 yards for a 12-pounder. The bigger the gun the larger the tin, and therefore the greater the number of musket balls inside it.

Finally there was the shell, a name we associate with a modern artillery piece, but it the 18th and 19th century it was merely one type of projectile. It was a hollow iron sphere containing a charge of gunpowder. A hole in it was plugged with a wooden fuse impregnated with an inflammable solution. This round was fired exclusively from howitzers and mortars, although the two varied considerably in size and appearance. Mortar shells often had lifting lugs in them, so they could be lowered into the mortar's mouth, and in mortars powder was usually loose, as the size of the charge needed could vary considerably. In howitzers, the shell was usually strapped to a wooden wad to form a sabot round.

When the shell was fired the fuse would be ignited. The burning time depended on the length of the fuse. When it burned through to the powder inside the sphere this ignited, blasting the shell apart. Then, fragments of red-hot metal would be blown among the ranks of the enemy. A variant was carcass shot, which was an incendiary round, used in sieges. When it disintegrated it scattered burning inflammable material around the target. When both 'common shells' and carcass shot were fired, they tended to be fused so they exploded on the ground, amid the ranks of the target. Then, around 1784, a British officer called Harry Shrapnel developed the spherical case shot, designed to explode in the air above the target after being fired from a howitzer. Shrapnel had deduced that the shell fragments fell with greater velocity thanks to gravity, and covered a smaller area, thereby concentrating the lethal effect of the blast.

This was fairly easy to achieve by fitting the shot with a shorter fuse. Shrapnel though, packed the spherical shell with musket balls, or rather slightly smaller carbine balls, which he felt were just as dangerous, and you could pack more of them into the space. Just enough room was left for the powder charge, which lay among the musket balls a bit like the sawdust did in a canister round. This meant the charge was smaller than normal, but Shrapnel overcame this by reducing the thickness of the hollow sphere's walls, and using the most volatile powder he could. In 1803 Shrapnel's shot was adopted for use by the British army, at least on a trial basis. It proved devastatingly effective, and earned the praise of the Duke of Wellington. So, from around 1809 it became issued without restriction. By the time the Napoleonic Wars ended other nations were considering adopting similar rounds for themselves. It was only in 1852 that the name spherical case shot was officially replaced by its more popular name, the Shrapnel shell.

Tactical innovation

Artillery tactics varied considerably during the Napoleonic period. Artillery could be used both offensively and defensively, and its role in a battle largely depended on the number of guns available, and the way the commanding general wanted the battle to develop. This in turn influenced the way guns would be used. For instance, one of the drawbacks of using artillery when advancing to the attack was that the field of fire of the batteries would be blocked by the advancing infantry. So, artillery tended to be sited on high ground, where it could fire over intervening troops, or else grouped on the flanks of the infantry formation. However, Napoleon favoured the bold handling of his guns when attacking. He often ordered them to advance to within a relatively short range of the enemy before unlimbering and opening fire. Often this was done in a series of rapid advances, designed eventually to place the enemy within canister range of the gun battery.

During his campaign against Prussia and Russia in 1806–07, Napoleon began grouping his guns together into massed batteries. At the battle of Wagram (1809) he gathered together a massed battery together to cover his flank, which allowed him to concentrate his infantry, forming an immense attack column which eventually punched its way through the Austrian line. This secured a hard-won French victory. This same reliance on massed gun batteries was seen at the battle of Borodino in 1812, and again at the battle of Waterloo three years later.

By contrast his opponent at Waterloo, the Duke of Wellington, favoured deploying his guns in individual batteries, ideally on a crest, while his infantry sheltered on its reverse slopes, where they were sheltered from enemy fire. The infantry could advance forward to support the guns, and if the gunners were attacked by cavalry they could leave their pieces and run back and shelter inside the infantry squares. For Wellington, guns were there to support his infantry and cavalry, while Napoleon, an artilleryman at heart, saw them as a weapon capable of winning a battle almost on their own, with the rest of his troops there to support his guns.

Guns at sea

It was with good reason that the 18th and early 19th centuries were known as 'The Age of Fighting Sail'. While guns were used on board ships before this, often very effectively, it was only in the later 17th century that fleets began to operate in a way that made the most out of their armament. By then the sailing warship had developed into a beautiful but deadly floating battery, with one, two or three decks of guns mounted inside its hull, the guns protruding from lines of gun ports cut in the ship's side. The trouble with this was that the guns had a very limited arc of fire – effectively they could only fire out to the side (or 'beam') of the ship. This meant that in order to operate effectively, fleets

British carronades in action during a naval engagement of the Napoleonic Wars. (Stratford Archive)

had to form battle lines, with one ship following the other, and where all the fleet's guns could bear on the enemy.

In this period ships were classified by 'rate', from the vast First Rates carrying 100 guns, to lowly Sixth Rates, which carried 24–30 pieces. First to Fourth Rate ships were deemed 'Ships-of-the-Line' – warships large enough to stand in the line of battle. However, by the 1790s the Fourth Rate (which carried 50–60 guns) was increasingly seen as too poorly armed to take on larger ships. So the most common ship-of-the-line of the period was a Third Rate, which officially carried 74 guns, or 37 on each broadside. In fact the armament of a nominal '74' varied slightly, as the carronade, a new type of gun, wasn't counted, and others were mounted as bow or stern chasers, rather than forming part of the broadside. To improve stability, the heaviest guns were carried on the lower gun deck, and increasingly lighter guns in any intermediate gun deck, or on the upper deck itself, depending if the ship was a one, two or three decker.

For the most part naval guns were the same as those used on land, although by this stage the majority were made from cast iron, while bronze guns remained the most common type for use ashore. However, the same four-wheeled truck carriages described earlier were still in use, as space remained at a premium on board. The difference was that gun weight was less important on board a ship. So, by 1800, most Fifth Rates (a ship type known as a 'frigate') carried 12-pounders and 18-pounders, while in ships of the line the main batteries consisted of 24-pounders and 36-pounders. Some of the largest First Rates carried even larger guns. This gave some individual warships a firepower that was greater than many field armies.

The carronade was developed exclusively for use at sea. First designed during the 1770s, it was a short, stumpy wide-bored gun, which could either fire a solid ball or a canister charge (known as 'grapeshot' at sea). These guns took up less space than conventional guns, and were mounted on carriages resembling the wheel-less sliding carriages used for garrison artillery pieces on land. However, they could fire a ball many times larger than a conventional gun of the same weight, or else an immense deadly round of grapeshot. The drawback with the canister was its range. Its effective range was around 400–700 yards, while a conventional long gun could pitch a ball more than mile. However, for a close-quarters fight it was a murderous killing machine, and rightly earned its nickname of 'the smasher'.

In terms of tactics, the 'line of battle' was more of a defensive than an offensive formation, and if both sides adopted it, then a sea battle could be inconclusive. For much of the 18th century admirals risked censure and even execution if they failed to form a line of battle, and so initiative was thwarted. That is why Vice-Admiral Horatio Nelson proved so successful. He realised that a decisive victory could only be achieved by abandoning these safe tactics and closing with the enemy. At the battle of Cape St. Vincent (1797) he ignored his orders and broke formation, to prevent a Spanish fleet from escaping. The following year at the battle of the Nile (1798) he attacked a line of French ships by dividing his fleet and assaulting them from both sides at once. Then, at Trafalgar in 1805, his fleet formed two columns, and closed with the enemy battle line, breaking it in two places, and so bringing about the greatest naval victory of the age.

Nelson realised that the battle line wasn't everything. By closing to point-blank range his ships could pass through the enemy line, firing into their unprotected bow or stern, then lying alongside the enemy and pouring shot into them faster than they could reply. He saw training, good gunnery, morale and discipline as the cornerstones of victory, not following the letter of his orders. He was fortunate in that the British enjoyed a superiority in gunnery during this period, mainly because their fleets were always at sea, practising for battle, while their blockaded French or Spanish counterparts were cooped up in port. So, he had the tools at his disposal to make the most of his wind-powered floating batteries. Naval guns and gunnery were the very cornerstone of Britain's naval supremacy.

CHAPTER 5

THE INDUSTRIAL AGE

1815–1914

THE END OF THE NAPOLEONIC WARS in 1815 brought a long period of peace to most of Europe, and this in turn led to the drastic scaling down of European armies. Small-scale wars were still being fought in Spain, North Africa, Greece and the Balkans and further afield in India, China or Central Asia, but these did little to upset the self-complacency that settled over the military establishment during this period. The war had encouraged technological and tactical innovation, and conversely this long period of peace stifled it. It would be almost four decades before major technological developments in artillery and ammunition would challenge the status quo, and even then conservative military chiefs tended to oppose change. Inevitably though, as the pace of innovation quickened, European powers were forced to adopt these new technological developments, or risk being left behind by their military rivals. During the second half of the 19th century the pace of this change became extremely rapid as gunners, innovators and ordnance designers all helped create the kind of artillery we know today.

The smooth-bore legacy

The Napoleonic era might not have been particularly noted for the technological development of artillery, but it was a period when the tactical use of guns received considerable attention, both on land and at sea. The decades that followed saw something of a retrenchment in both areas. This was understandable – the general peace in Europe meant that there was little impetus behind the development of artillery, while commanders tended to stick with the tactics that served them well during these past wars. This said, during the decades which followed Napoleon's defeat at Waterloo (1815) were marked by a number of artillery innovations and experiments which collectively laid the foundations for the great developments which would follow.

During the Napoleonic Wars small easily transportable guns had been developed for use in mountainous terrain. The British especially made use of these 'mountain guns' during their advance through the Pyrenees in 1813, and again during their intervention in the Spanish Carlist Wars of the 1830s. The small 3-pounder guns were light enough to be carried by mules, while their carriages could also be dismantled and transported the same way. As a result they were labelled 'pack' guns, as they could be easily broken down into small packages of barrel, carriage, wheels, tools and ammunition. In various forms these pack guns remained a staple of British ordnance throughout the 19th century, proving particularly useful during Queen Victoria's 'little wars' in Africa, India and Central Asia.

In general the 18th century had witnessed a gradual reduction in the decoration applied to artillery. This trend continued into the 19th century, until for the most part artillery had a utilitarian and streamlined look, where function was considered far more important than appearance. This in turn led to a general standardisation of appearance across Europe. The exception was when various ordnance experts developed their own variants of existing artillery patterns, or designed barrels to suit a new type of ammunition. For example, after the Napoleonic wars the French artillery general Henri-Joseph Paixhans developed a type of gun capable of firing an explosive shell. Until then only howitzers could use this kind of ammunition, using indirect fire. The Paixhans gun, which underwent its first trials in 1821, was designed to fire shells on a flat trajectory.

The implication of this was particularly noticeable at sea, as warships of the period were built from wood. Now, artillery had the ability to fire at a wooden-hulled ship and set it on fire. On land, Paixhans shells had a greater destructive power than iron round shot, and greatly increased the effectiveness of field artillery. Despite these tactical advantages bureaucratic delays and production problems meant that the French didn't begin phasing in these new guns and shells until 1837. Two years later the British followed suit. The difference was, the British used shells as an alternative to round shot, while the French gradually abandoned solid non-explosive projectiles. It wouldn't be until the late 1850s that the switch from round shot to shells would be made in most of Europe, which meant that for almost two decades, the French were ahead of the game.

In Britain howitzers had largely been used as siege guns. However, in 1820 a new type of iron howitzer was developed by a General Miller, for use in the field. At the other end of the scale, during the early 1840s Colonel William Dundas of the Royal Artillery developed a pattern of large cast-iron 68-pounder smooth-bore guns for coastal defence, but it was soon adopted by the navy. In line with British ordnance policy at the time it could fire both solid round shot and Paixhans shells, as well as canister rounds, which made it as versatile as it was reliable. During the Crimean War (1853–56) these guns were even landed from ships and used as siege weapons. This represented an advance in heavy ordnance that paved the way for the following generation of large siege guns and naval pieces.

Meanwhile in the France of the 1830s the inventor Guilliaume Piobert scientifically tested the effectiveness of siege guns by battering obsolete Vauban fortifications with them using both shot and shell. By the 1840s this had led to a more methodical approach to siegecraft, where a combination of round shot and shells proved highly effective in reducing fortifications. It wasn't just the guns and ammunition that received attention – new developments also changed the way guns were fired. For centuries guns had been fired by setting off a priming charge in the cannon's vent, which led from the touchhole to the main charge sitting in the breech of the gun. The only modification introduced during the later 18th century was the use of a flammable quill in the vent, which was less vulnerable to rain or damp than loose powder. Then, in the early 1820s, the Reverend Alexander Forsyth developed the percussion cap. While this was invented as an ignition system for sporting rifles, it would eventually be used to fire artillery too.

Since the mid-18th century, naval guns had been fired using one of two methods – a gunlock or using a piece of burning slowmatch. The advantage of the gunlock was that ignition was faster and more reliable. However, some gun captains stuck to the old ways, or used both systems, in case a gunlock should fail. These gunlocks were flintlocks, virtually identical to the flintlock ignition systems used in contemporary muskets. On land, most nations stuck to the more old-fashioned slowmatch. The gunlock system relied on a flint striking a metal plate to create a spark, so igniting a small pool of loose gunpowder in the pan – the priming charge. With Forsyth's system, the flint was replaced by a percussion cap made from fulminate of mercury, enclosed in a brass container or cap. It fitted over a hollow steel nipple, and when activated a hammer would strike the cap, thus creating a spark. The spark would travel down the hollow cavity inside the nipple to ignite the priming charge.

It was an all-weather ignition system, and far more reliable than the older gunlock. However, it took time to convince the military forces of the world to embrace this new invention. Consequently it would be the mid-1840s before the percussion system was used in military muskets and artillery pieces. It was the British who led the way – in 1838 a percussion tube was adopted for use in the Royal Navy. It consisted of a small copper tube filled with gunpowder. At one end was a percussion cap, and a hook for a lanyard. this was inserted into the gun's vent, and when the lanyard was pulled the percussion cap would detonate, setting off the charge in the tube, which in turn ignited the powder charge inside the gun. It proved highly successful at sea, and the same system was adopted by the British army seven years later. However, it was soon replaced by a simpler 'friction tube' or 'friction primer', which used abrading metal surfaces to create a spark instead. These were in widespread use throughout Europe and the Americas by the start of the 1860s.

Despite all these developments, these guns were still smooth-bored weapons. In the navy, innovations such as the Dundas smooth-bore, sighting mechanisms, improved gun carriages and friction tubes had certainly improved the power, accuracy and performance of naval guns, but essentially they remained the same weapons which had seen service at Trafalgar. Similarly the British, French, Turkish or Russian guns used during the Crimean War were little different from the ordnance used by Napoleon. That though, was about to change, with the development of a reliable rifled breech-loading gun.

Rifling and breech-loaders

Being the largest European war for three decades the Crimean War proved something of a turning point, as it revealed the limitations of smooth-bore guns. The smooth-bores of 1855 were no more accurate than those of forty years earlier, and although experiments into rifled guns had been carried out, the military establishment of Europe were extremely resistant to change. In the end the inevitable move from smooth-bores to rifled guns came about thanks to technological developments that were the direct result of Henri-Joseph Paixhans' new ordnance.

The Crimean War began with a war between Russia and Turkey. Britain and France then entered the conflict to limit the spread of Russian power in the Balkans. The vulnerability of Turkey was demonstrated in 1853 when the Russian navy demolished its Turkish counterpart in the battle of Sinope. Although both sides had similar ships, the Russian warships carried new Paixhans guns, which proved devastatingly effective against Turkey's wooden-hulled fleet. During the war, Britain, France, Turkey and Russia all relied on steam-powered wooden warships, but the French also pioneered the use of floating batteries, protected by iron plates. These proved the forerunners for a new kind of iron-clad warship, the first ocean-going example of which was the French *La Gloire*, which was launched in 1859. Britain responded with its own ironclad, HMS *Warrior*, which was launched the following year. These ironclad warships transformed naval warfare.

Shells from a Paixhans gun would just explode harmlessly against the armoured side of these new warships. It was clear that a new kind of gun or projectile would be needed to counter the rise of the ironclad. Fortunately the mid-19th century was a time when inventiveness flourished, and ordnance designers came up with a number of innovative solutions. Some of these were more successful than others. In Britain Charles Lancaster invented an oval-bored gun that was designed to impart spin to the projectile. When his 68-pounder guns were used in the Crimea it was found the shells tended to stick in the bore. Then there was Mallet's Mortar, an equally large weapon designed to rain enormous 2,400-pound explosive shells down on the defences of Sevastopol. The war ended before this enormous mortar could be shipped out to the Crimea.

Surprisingly, the Russians found that solid iron round shot was more useful against ironclad floating batteries, as the concussion they caused when striking the iron proved more destructive than the explosive power of more modern shells. However, while this discovery was reinforced by the experiences of both sides when fighting ironclad warships during the American Civil War (1861–65), a more efficient solution lay in developing a round with enough power to punch its way through the ship's armour. This meant creating a gun which would give a shell enough velocity to do just that. As powerful as large smooth-bore guns were, they were cudgels, when what was needed was a gun that could fire daggers capable of piercing the protective armour of the target. The solution was the rifled gun.

Hand-held rifled weapons had been around since the later 18th century, used mainly as hunting rifles, but also increasingly as infantry firearms. The idea of the rifled barrel was to impart a spin on the round when it was fired. This meant that the projectile would keep turning when it was in flight which greatly improved both its range and accuracy. While this worked for small-arms, the development of an effective rifled artillery piece was a much tougher proposition thanks to the scale of the gun, and the difficulties of accurately rifling the inside of a large cast-metal barrel. In France, the artillery officer Antoine Treuille de Beaulieu made a detailed study of rifling during the 1840s, and came up with a rifling system based on the cutting of six shallow spiralling grooves in the barrel of a bronze muzzle-loading gun. At the same time Baron Wahrendorff in Sweden and Major Cavalli in Italy came up with similar systems, but couldn't quite get them to work. So, it was the French who made the real breakthrough.

De Beaulieu's shell had zinc studs on it, which when fired would spiral through the grooves and on towards the target. Thanks to the spin, the nose of the shell always hit the target first. That meant the base of the shell could be fused, to control when a high-explosive shell could be detonated – either while in flight, when it hit something or just after impact. By 1858 the La Hitte system was adopted by the French army, named after the general of ordnance who implemented the introduction of these rifled guns. After some deliberation the French navy followed suit. These new weapons proved their worth in the Franco-Austrian War of 1859, which in turn led to other countries taking an interest in these developments. One of the lessons the Austrians learned from their defeats at Solferino and Magenta was that their artillery was inferior to that of the French. Consequently they adopted their own rifled system, and during the Austro-Prussian War (1866) these guns proved superior to their Prussian counterparts.

Britain's answer to de Beaulieu was an industrialist called William Armstrong. Having followed military developments in the Crimea he wrote to the Secretary of State for War, suggesting that he could design and built a light rifled field gun which could outshoot the Russian batteries. He was commissioned to build six guns, and in 1856 he presented them for evaluation. Armstrong had designed his gun in a radically new way. Instead of using cast iron he reverted to wrought iron – the gun material used in the medieval period – and built guns along broadly similar lines to these early pieces. A steel barrel was reinforced by compressed wrought-iron bands, their thickness engineered precisely to absorb the explosive pressure expected at that part of the gun barrel. This made the guns noticeably fatter round the breech than at the barrel. Internally the bore was rifled with shallow and very gradually spiralling grooves, while the shell itself was coated in lead. When the gun was fired the soft lead would expand into grooves, and the round would spiral as it left the barrel.

What really set Armstrong's 3-pounder rifled guns apart though, was their breech. Unlike all other rifled guns, his were breech-loading weapons. Again, this was a throwback to the chambered guns of the medieval period. The difference was that both wrought-iron technology and the engineering of artillery breeches had moved on since the 15th century. Armstrong's gun ended in a thick metal block, which was screwed into the back of the gun's breech. This formed a tight seal, and was easy to operate. His guns proved a success, although the steel inner bore was less than ideal, and in his later designs Armstrong replaced it with a wrought-iron rifled sleeve. The guns were accepted by the Board

An Armstrong 110-pounder breech-loading gun, on the gundeck of HMS Warrior *(1860), now preserved as a historic ship in Portsmouth. (Stratford Archive)*

of Ordnance in 1858, and the following year Armstrong was appointed Engineer for rifled ordnance to the War Department.

By the time Britain's first ironclad HMS *Warrior* entered service in 1861 she carried a battery of powerful Armstrong 110-pounder (7-inch) rifled breech-loading guns (or RBLs in contemporary military parlance). These guns had a range of around 2 miles, and a muzzle velocity of over 1,000 feet per second. In the Armstrong the Royal Navy had a weapon capable of fighting and sinking *La Gloire*. The gun though, wasn't without criticism. A breech blew out during the naval bombardment of a Japanese port in 1864, which demonstrated that the gun's complex breech mechanism was prone to mishandling in the heat of an action. However, it was lauded for its impressive range, accuracy and penetrative power. Regardless of critics, the rifled gun was here to stay, and it looked like the breech-loader was too.

In Germany, gun manufacture was dominated by Alfred Krupp, whose cast-steel guns were adopted by the Prussian army in 1859. The press dubbed him the 'Cannon King', and despite

A 9cm Krupp breech-loading gun, of the kind used by the Prussian Army during the Franco-Prussian War. (Stratford Archive)

the poor showing of his guns during the Austro-Prussian War his weapons were exported throughout the world. He perfected their design, and so during the Franco-Prussian War (1870–71) his German breech-loading guns consistently out-ranged and out-performed their muzzle-loading French counterparts. During the war Krupp continued to supply the army with what it needed, and so during the siege of Paris in 1871 he provided them with light guns to shoot down French aerial balloons. These were arguably the world's first anti-aircraft guns.

While Armstrong favoured producing guns from wrought iron, Alfred Krupp used steel, strengthened using the Bessemer process, which was first invented in 1856. With the benefit of hindsight we would assume that steel barrels represented the future of artillery, but in these innovative later decades of the 19th century Armstrong's wrought-iron guns looked every bit as promising as the ordnance being designed by Krupp. Also, in Britain, Armstrong wasn't the only manufacturer of rifled guns. Another engineering manufacturer, Joseph Whitworth, perfected a steel breech-loading rifled gun, which was rejected by the Board of Ordnance, but his 12-pounder gun went on to see service during the American Civil War. It was an exceptionally accurate gun, but its complicated breech mechanism was prone to jamming, and in America its special hexagonal projectiles had to be imported, and so were in short supply. By contrast the sliding mechanism adopted by Krupp was simple to operate, and would set the standard for the next generation of breech-loading guns.

While breech-loading systems had their critics, rifled guns proved their worth during the American Civil War. The majority of guns in Union or Confederate service were 12-pounder muzzle-loading smooth-bores known as 'Napoleons' as they were designed according to a pattern developed by Emperor Napoleon III of France. While these guns proved effective, the conflict demonstrated that in everything but rate of fire, rifled guns were far superior. Their range and accuracy was significantly greater than that of the Napoleons, and while the number and make of rifled guns varied, almost all of them proved as reliable as they were effective. Rifled guns designed by Charles James proved less than ideal, as their deep rifling grooves meant smouldering fragments of cartridge could get lodged inside their barrels, which in turn increased the risk of accidental discharge. Still, the James rifle remained in use throughout the war.

A slightly better piece was those designed by Robert Parrot of the West Point Foundry, His 10-pounder and 20-pounder Parrot rifles though, had a propensity to rupture after extensive use, the barrel bursting just in front of the thick reinforcing band that encircled the breech. Understandably this made them unpopular with gunners. Much more reliable was the 3-inch Ordnance Rifle designed by Thomas Rodman. Its smooth slightly bulbous barrel was reliable, largely because Rodman had based its design on thoroughly scientific principles. All these

Union guns in action at the battle of Stones River (Murfreesbro),
American Civil War, c. 1863. (Stratford Archive)

pieces though, were muzzle-loaders rather than breech-loaders. They were also slightly less effective than Napoleons when firing canister, thanks to their narrower bore. Still, their performance impressed foreign observers so much that by 1865 it was clear that rifled guns represented the future of artillery.

The trouble was, across Europe most countries still had large stocks of smooth-bore guns, and were naturally reluctant to get rid of them. The obvious solution was to re-bore them so they could accept rifled shells. Some countries did this the old-fashioned way, using metalworkers to physically chisel grooves into the barrels of guns. In Britain a much better system was proposed by Captain William Palliser, who suggested boring out existing guns and then inserting a steel liner with three rifling grooves in it. The Board of Ordnance approved the idea, and soon hundreds of old guns had been re-bored to fit the Palliser system. This was particularly cost-effective when it came to those heavy guns used in coastal defence, or by the larger warships of the Royal Navy. Soon a similar system was adopted elsewhere in Europe. This though, meant that muzzle-loading guns continued to outnumber breech-loading pieces. In Britain and elsewhere, this led to an attempt to reverse the course of progress.

The rifled muzzle-loader

In July 1870, a decision was made which halted development in Britain for a decade. A committee of British artillery officers formed a committee to evaluate two new guns – a 9-pounder steel rifled breech-loader (RBL) and a 9-pounder bronze rifled muzzle-loader (RML). The committee selected the RML, as they felt it was more versatile and reliable. At the time Britain was involved in near-incessant colonial wars, and these factors were deemed of vital importance in the kind of low-intensity fighting being waged in Africa and Northern India in the name of Queen Victoria. This tipped the scales in the Board of Ordnance, and so while no new RBLs were accepted for a decade, the production of RMLs was accelerated.

This was a strange decision, coming as the superiority of Prussian breech-loading Krupp guns was being demonstrated on the battlefields of France. The French bronze muzzle-loaders lacked the range and rate of fire of their Prussian counterparts, and while this point was noted by most foreign military observers during the Franco-Prussian War, the British preferred to follow their own path. While bronze RMLs still in service continued to be used, any new guns of this kind would be made from steel and wrought iron using the Armstrong principle. Ironically in 1871 Armstrong resigned from his post in protest at the decision to abandon breech loading. While he continued his own private development of breech-loading guns, others began building a new generation of RMLs, for use in the field, at sea or in coastal fortifications. Britain's example was followed by others, at least until more reliable breech-loading systems could be designed.

As if to underline the point, in 1872 a Prussian 9-pounder steel RBL was tested next to a British 9-pounder iron RML. The evaluators felt the Prussian gun was more accurate, but the British one had a longer range, and was easier to use. This wasn't strictly a fair comparison, as it used an older breech mechanism – the Prussian army had modified theirs after their war with France. Still, the British gun was good – a similar experiment carried out in France led the French team to declare them to be as good as any gun then in service anywhere in Europe. In the years that followed the 9-pounder was followed by an 18-pounder 'position gun', and then a 13-pounder RML to replace the earlier 9-pounder. RMLs also appeared in the siege train, in coastal defences and at sea, with earlier RBLs including the 110-pounder Armstrong gun being replaced by 25-, 40- and 64-pounder RMLs. At the same time an 8-inch RML howitzer replaced existing mortars and howitzers in the British siege train.

In fact the 1870s and early 1880s marked the heyday of the rifled muzzle-loader. The principal concern of the Royal Navy was how to combat the growing number of ironclads in the fleets of potential rivals. The solution was to build increasingly large and powerful RMLs, both for use in ships and as coastal artillery pieces. Inevitably this led to the construction of enormous guns – the most powerful artillery pieces ever seen at that time. These were large, ugly bottle-shaped weapons, with thick reinforcing bands surrounding their breech to cope with the incredibly large explosive charges these guns required. So, the 12.5-inch RML used in the Royal Navy and in coastal batteries weighed 38 tons, and fired a Palliser shell weighing over 800 pounds. With its full propellant charge of 200 pounds of powder, this gun's shells had a velocity of more than 1,500 feet per second. This meant that at a range of 1,000 yards its shells could penetrate 18 inches of iron plate. At last the navy had a gun capable of sinking any ironclad afloat.

That, of course, wasn't the end of it. Naval architects and steel manufacturers like Krupp found ways to make a warship's armoured plating thicker, stronger and more impervious. Consequently the gun designers produced larger guns. In 1881 HMS *Inflexible* entered service, armed with four 80-ton RMLs, in two large turrets, while in Italy the two ironclads of the Caio Duilio class mounted 100-ton RMLs, bought from Armstrong's factory. The trouble was, muzzle-loading guns of this size were almost too large to reload. Even then the process involved hydraulic rammers, specially built shell hoists and a great deal of time and labour. As a result the rate of fire dropped to one round every four or five minutes – three times slower than the 38-ton RML. Effectively, this meant that at least at sea, RMLs had become too large to be practicable. As a result, the Admiralty began to consider a return to breech-loading weapons.

HMS *Inflexible* wasn't the last British warship armed with RMLs. Four more large turret ships were still under construction, and these entered service between 1883 and 1887. However, in 1879 a 12-inch RML on board HMS *Thunderer* was accidentally double-loaded, and it burst, killing ten men and injuring many more. Critics rightly pointed out that this sort of accident couldn't have happened if the gun had been a breech-loader. So, in 1880, when the Admiralty ordered a new capital ship, it decided to arm it with breech-loading guns rather than muzzle-loaders. This ship, HMS *Collingwood*, would be the first of a long line of capital ships to be built that deserved the more modern description of 'battleship' rather than 'ironclad'. Twenty years before, HMS *Warrior*, the most powerful ironclad in the world, was protected by 4½ inches of wrought-iron plate, with another 18 inches of wooden backing. By contrast, along its hull, *Collingwood* was protected by a steel belt 18 inches thick. This new type of battleship deserved an equally new type of gun. So *Collingwood* was designed to carry four 12-inch breech-loading guns, mounted in two barbettes – a form of open-topped gun turret. These pieces, designed in Woolwich, were the first truly modern battleship guns in the world. They were constructed by screwing a breech-block onto the end of a long steel tube, and then wrapping the barrel in three coiled layers of metal – the first of carbon steel, the second of mild steel, and then the outer one of wrought iron. The coils stopped 8 feet from the end of the 25-foot-long barrel, while a wrought-iron jacket covered its whole length. This essentially represented the state of the art of gunfounding in the 1880s, and was a system that would be followed with minor variations in all subsequent large battleship guns. While these 12-inch breech-loading (BL) guns Mark I had problems, and needed to be redesigned, the Mark II version proved reliable – and superior in every way to RMLs of the same size. So, as far as the Royal Navy was concerned, the RML was consigned to obsolescence.

By then the British Army had reached the same conclusion. In late 1878 the Director of Artillery noted that as guns had become longer, a return to breech-loading was inevitable. He pointed out that in Germany Krupp had designed a breech mechanism which used a sliding block mechanism, which proved much more effective than his older system which had seen service in the Franco-Prussian War. The French had recently adopted an interrupted screw mechanism, which proved very efficient, while in Britain the Whitworth continuous screw method was superior to older Armstrong breech mechanisms of a decade earlier. He advocated an evaluation of all these mechanisms, and the adoption of one of them for all new British guns. Meanwhile the British Admiralty hadn't waited for the Board of Ordnance to carry out its evaluation. It merely wanted the best breech mechanisms available at the time a new battleship was ready to receive her guns. As a result a combination of systems were introduced, before the board finally approved the interrupted thread system.

The interrupted thread or interrupted screw system used in breech-loaders was first pioneered in France during the 1840s, but it was never fully developed until after the Franco-Prussian War. Until the war, the French army relied on RMLs, as its

HMS Inflexible *(1876) carried four 80-ton RMLs, mounted in two twin turrets. (Stratford Archive)*

ordnance experts felt that there was no reliable breech-loading mechanism available. Following France's defeat a French artillery officer, Colonel Charles de Bange, proposed a new way of sealing a breech-loading gun. His system relied on an obturating ring – a large washer like a plumber's 'O' ring whose soft asbestos surface expanded due to the pressure when a gun was fired, sealing the breech as it did so. This though, was only part of his solution. The ring sat at the end of a breech block which was fitted with a screw thread. This block was hinged, so when the shell was loaded it could be swung into place, and by turning a lever the thread would engage with threads in the inside of the barrel.

The obturating ring then sat between the breech block and the end of the barrel. When the gun was fired the ring sealed the barrel perfectly. To reload, all the gunners needed to do was to pull on their lever, and swing the breech block open again. While the system itself looked dauntingly complex, the basics of it were straightforward enough, and it was simple and quick to use. De Bange was given an official position and the resources he needed to develop his system, and as a result, in 1877, the French produced their first modern breech-loading gun, the

De Bange 90-mm gun. The gun proved highly successful, and demonstrated the effectiveness of the de Bange system. Foreign observers were quick to pick up on the efficiency of de Bange's system, and so when the British Admiralty were looking for a system to use in *Collingwood*'s 12-inch guns, they opted for their own version of de Bange's mechanism. They realised that this represented the future for artillery.

Perfecting the breech-loader

De Bange's innovations was just one of a number of developments which revolutionised the artillery of the later 19th century. For the past few decades ballistics experts had been able to accurately determine the velocity of a shell, and the flight taken by projectiles. Since the 1860s they could also accurately monitor pressure inside a gun barrel, which meant gun designers had the hard information they needed to create safe and efficient artillery pieces. This in turn allowed scientists to work out how efficient gunpowder was, and to come up with new and more efficient types of propellant. Until then, gunpowder had largely remained unchanged since the 17th century.

It was William Armstrong who first tried to find a powder that burned more slowly than regular black powder, which in turn would make the engaging of his shells in a barrel's rifling more effective. His solution was to introduce large grain powder, which burned at a slightly slower rate, and therefore developed its full explosive power a little more gradually. In America, Thomas Rodman went a step further, adding more charcoal to the mix. This in turn led to a range of different powders of varying composition and grains, for different sizes and types of guns. Meanwhile in Austria and Germany, guncotton was developed as an alternative. However, this cotton impregnated with nitroglycerine proved unstable, and it was the Austrian Baron Wilhelm von Lenk who finally worked out how to stabilise it during experiments conducted in the 1860s. It didn't prove a satisfactory propellant though, so the idea was shelved. It was resurrected at the end of the century when it was used as a charge for mines and torpedoes.

Meanwhile, in 1865 the Prussian artillery officer Johann Schultz developed a type of gunpowder which was smokeless. The advantage was obvious – gun smoke betrayed the position of artillery batteries on the battlefield, but by using smokeless powder their location would be much harder to detect. However, his mix of nitro-lignose and saltpetre proved too violent a charge for rifled guns. So, it was the French who first developed a reliable type of smokeless powder, which they called 'Poudre B'. Other countries soon followed their lead, and by the 1880s smokeless powder had become the standard form of propellant for modern artillery pieces, both on land and at sea. The Swedish scientist Alfred Nobel perfected the mixture when he produced bauxite in 1887, and two years later the British – one of the last military powers to embrace these changes – switched to their own version, which they called cordite.

Projectiles underwent a makeover too. While earlier in the century there was simply shot, shell, canister or shrapnel, by the 1880s old-fashioned round shot was no longer used, and shells of various kind were used for everything. William Armstrong was the first to experiment with one-piece rounds containing the shell and a cartridge case containing the propellant, but his 'segment shell' was not a success. More useful was his introduction of time fuses, fitted into the nose of his shells. This allowed high-explosive (HE) rounds or 'common shells' to be set to burst at set ranges – creating a more effective anti-personnel round and effectively negating the need for canister. Shrapnel shells were re-configured to fit rifled guns, and when fitted with a similar time fuse these became even more deadly than before. Finally, to penetrate the armour of an enemy warship, armour-piercing (AP) rounds were created, designed to explode after smashing their way through the side of an armoured warship.

The other great innovation of the late 19th century was the re-invention of the howitzer. Before the advent of rifling these had been reasonably effective siege weapons. On the battlefield, their ability to fire shrapnel also made them useful anti-personnel guns. Rifling extended their range, but that in turn made their fire harder to control. Then, following the poor performance of Russian siege guns during the Russo-Turkish War (1877–78), a Russian artillery officer published a treatise advocating the scientific use of indirect fire. The problem, he argued, was the inability of gunners to accurately calculate the best trajectory for their shot using existing gunnery tools. Then, around 1890 the Germans developed an azimuth sight which solved the problem. It was attached to the howitzer, the sight aligned with the barrel. Equipped with this sight, an inclinometer and a set of published trajectory tables a howitzer crew could work out roughly where their shell would land. Other nations soon copied the German innovation, and howitzers, regarded as largely ineffective in 1877, now resumed their place as one of the most useful weapons on the battlefield. This innovation opened up a whole new world of indirect fire for artillerymen.

Now, gunners could harness the increasing range of modern rifled howitzers to target a distant enemy hidden behind fortifications or in trenches with a fair degree of accuracy. This required the howitzers firing a shell with a steep angle of ascent, which would then plunge down on the target. If fitted with a timed fuse it would explode in the air in a burst of shrapnel. Otherwise it would hit the target and explode there. In either case this new type of gunnery required a thoroughly scientific approach, and a degree of mathematical precision. The result though was to transform the way artillery would be used. In the next chapter we will see how indirect fire soon became the standard way guns were used on the battlefield. For now though, the ability to pound the enemy from a relatively safe distance meant that the days of the field gun were now numbered.

This was a period of rapid technological change, and the primitive *mitrailleuse* machine guns used in the Franco-Prussian War were soon replaced by more efficient hand-cranked Gatling, Gardner and Nordenfeldt machine guns, which in British service proved invaluable in colonial actions fought in Africa and in India's northern frontiers. Then, in 1880 the Royal Navy bought a number of Nordenfeldt 1-inch guns. The aim was to use them to protect warships from torpedo boats. The French firm Hotchkiss then produced an even more powerful 37-mm version. What set these light guns apart was their ammunition, and their rate of fire. They fired solid shells, but these were joined to a disposable brass cartridge case which contained the propellant and its own firing pin. In effect it was a larger version of the rifle ammunition then entering service. These little breech-loading guns could fire 15 rounds a minute, and this, combined with their simple one-piece projectiles earned them the apt description of Quick Firing (QF) guns.

Soon, QF guns were adapted for use on land – the first being a Russian weapon, which entered service in 1887. However it was the French who really developed QF guns for their army, and their results are described in the next chapter. What did find widespread approval though, was the notion that rather than loading the shell and then the powder charges separately into the breech of a gun, it was faster and more efficient to join the two into one combined body, containing both shell and a disposable metal cartridge case. This was only possible where the gun calibre was small enough and the shell light enough to be easily manhandled. However, it would take time for this idea to gain widespread acceptance. More pressing was the problem of finding a thoroughly reliable way of firing guns, and then finding a way to cope with the problem of recoil.

The first problem was relatively straightforward. By the 1860s most guns were fired using a friction tube attached to a lanyard. By then though, considerable advances had been made in electricity, and in 1855 an electric tube was developed in the

British ordnance centre at Woolwich. In 1866 this service electric tube was adopted for test firings, but the army was resistant to change. By contrast the Admiralty immediately recognised the potential of the system, as it created the possibility of a whole ship's main armament being fired simultaneously, using one electrical impulse. Similarly the US Army adopted their own electrical tube, called a 'primer'. The friction tube though, remained in general use well into the 20th century, thanks to its simplicity and reliability.

Recoil was a far more serious problem. Every time a gun fired the blast pushed the gun and carriage backwards. At sea this recoil was checked by the use of breech ropes which secured the gun to the side of the ship. In coastal batteries, the carriage itself recoiled on the inclined slope of a lower carriage, which helped absorb most of the recoil. In Britain, some coastal batteries harnessed this force by mounting their guns on a Moncrieff Disappearing Carriage. When the gun fired, a hinged carriage used the force of the recoil to swing backwards and down, reaching a position where it could be reloaded below the parapet of the fort. This was ingenious, but it wasn't a solution. After firing on land, the gun had to be manhandled back into place, and the range and elevation of the piece recalibrated before it could be fired again. The solution was to find some way to absorb this recoil, so that the gun stayed where it was after firing.

In 1881 the British Army was issued with a 12-pounder RBL, which proved to be an excellent gun, apart from its weight and the tendency of its carriage to recoil with considerable force. So, a new recoil carriage was developed, which was retro-fitted to the gun in 1890. It performed so well it was dubbed 'The Elastic Field Gun'. The way it worked was quite simple. The top section of the steel gun carriage had a recoil cylinder fitted to it, which sat inside a slide in the lower portion of the carriage. Inside it was a piston rod and a series of powerful springs. Now when the gun fired the piston hit the springs, and all but 4 inches of the force was absorbed. To absorb the remainder of the recoil, the lower carriage was fitted with a self-acting brake. This ingenious system became the basis for a new generation of recoil-absorbing gun mountings.

It soon became clear that a hydraulic cylinder was the key to the recoil problem. A liquid-filled cylinder in the carriage was linked to a piston attached to the underside of the gun itself. When the gun recoiled the liquid would absorb the movement and energy created. Once this 'hydraulic buffer' had done its work, either springs or gravity would return the barrel to its original firing position. Often two or more sets of cylinders and springs were used. The trouble was, while larger guns mounted on ships or in coastal batteries had the space to house these hydraulic buffers and springs, smaller field guns did not. Eventually lighter hydraulic buffers would enter service, but in the meantime a partial solution was to fit spades to the end of the gun carriage, sometime equipped with springs, which would transfer most of the force of the recoil into the ground. It was 1897 when the French finally solved the problem, and so created the first of the truly modern field guns described in the next chapter.

This era saw more change in the world of artillery than in any other historical period before or since. The artillery pieces of the 1840s and early 1850s were almost exclusively smooth-bored muzzle-loading weapons, little different from the guns of the Napoleonic Wars. In fact, a time-travelling gunner from the 16th century would have little problem firing a gun during the Crimean War. Then the whole world of gunnery was turned on its head, first by the introduction of rifling, and then breech-loading. While the technological development of artillery didn't always follow a smooth road, the general trend was towards ever more powerful and efficient guns. A succession of innovations overcame most of the problems facing artillerymen during this period, until both on land and sea, ordnance became a deadly reflection of the industrial might and ingenuity of the age. This development led to the creation of a thoroughly modern artillery piece that with a few variations would be used throughout two world wars, and which is still in use today.

CHAPTER 6

WORLD WAR I

1914–1918

THE CREATION OF THE QUICK FIRER was the real breakthrough that transformed the world of artillery. The use of fixed one-piece ammunition made loading and firing much faster, and this, combined with other developments like hydraulic buffers, reliable breech mechanisms and new types of ammunition all added to the gunnery revolution that took place at the end of the 19th century. Artillery designers tried to incorporate all these new improvements in their latest designs, but the speed of change was so fast that newly introduced guns were in danger of becoming outdated before they had even been fully tested on the battlefield. Also, many European armies were resistant to change – after all their existing guns worked perfectly well – or so they thought. Financial constraints, and the belief that new designs would be too complicated for artillerymen to operate, conspired to stem the tide of progress. Then, in the late 1890s, two things happened which would show that change wasn't only inevitable – it was vitally necessary.

Fin de siècle

The first of these events was the introduction of a new French field gun. In 1897 the French 75-mm Quick-Firing Gun entered service, a weapon capable of firing 20 rounds per minute when operated by a well-trained crew. It was accurate too, thanks largely to its improved hydraulic recoil system. The gun carriage would remain perfectly still when it fired, which meant the gun layer had little need to re-adjust his point of aim. One-piece ammunition with combined steel shell and brass cartridge case had already been used in other quick firers, but the French had improved theirs, so it was now more reliable, and used smokeless powder. To cap it all the crew was protected by a bullet-proof steel gun shield, which was important given the current range of modern small arms. Effectively the French 75-mm gun made all other field guns appear old-fashioned. It was the first new gun of a new age. While other leading military powers took stock of this development, a small colonial war in South Africa was beginning – a conflict that would grow in intensity, and would demonstrate both the strength and the vulnerability of modern artillery.

At first the British regarded the Second Boer War (1899–1902) as just another in a long line of minor colonial conflicts. Their complacency led to a string of defeats at the hands of the Boer 'Commandos' – military units formed largely of hardy Afrikaaner farmers who used their skill on horseback and with the rifle to discomfit the British regulars. The fledgling Boer republics were also armed with artillery, ranging from small 37-mm quick firers and German Krupp or French Schneider-Cruesot field guns to large 155-mm Cruesot siege guns. For their part the British relied on 12-pounder and 15-pounder RBLs, and the 5-inch BL howitzer, supported at times by 4.7-inch naval guns landed from warships and fitted with land carriages. During the war the Boer guns consistently out-performed the British ones, both in terms of range and accuracy.

British Artillery in action at the battle of Colenso (1899). (Stratford Archive)

At the battle of Colenso (1899) the Boer guns were concealed in makeshift emplacements, and with their smokeless powder the British had problems locating them. In contrast the British guns were deployed on an open plain, where their gun crews were easily picked off by long-range snipers, or the guns wrecked by counter-battery fire. The British guns lacked gun shields, and so their crews were vulnerable to enemy fire. It was only later in the war, after the British rethought their artillery tactics, that their guns enjoyed some success. They were increasingly used to laying down heavy bombardments on Boer positions, just before the British infantry were sent in. Ultimately this kind of infantry–artillery cooperation would stand the British in good stead during World War I. Other lessons learned included the sighting of guns in concealed positions, and the ability to direct artillery fire even though the gunners couldn't see the target.

After the war the British were forced to re-equip their army with more modern field guns. As an interim measure they went to Germany and bought 15-pounder QF guns from the

A French 75-mm QF Model 1897 in action, World War I. (Chronicle/Alamy)

Ehrhardt ordnance factory in Germany. These guns had a fully recoiling carriage, the first in British service, but these were complex, while the guns themselves, formed from a solid ingot of metal, were also unusual. They proved excellent guns, and the first true quick-firing weapons in the British army, but for political reasons a home-made version was deemed necessary. Eventually, after seemingly endless committee meetings and discussion the Board of Ordnance opted for two guns, a 13-pounder for the horse artillery, and an 18-pounder for other field batteries. These new guns combined wire-bound steel barrels designed by Armstrong, a recoil system built by Vickers, and the latest sighting and elevating devices produced by the Royal Ordnance factory.

These guns were both deemed excellent in tests conducted in 1903, and by the following year they began entering service, while the 15-pounder Ehrhardt guns were handed over to the reserve gunners of the Territorial Army. The 18-pounder Field Gun Mark I had a range of 6,500 yards (3.6 miles), while with

A German 77-mm FK97 nA field gun. (Stratford Archive)

a calibre of 84 mm its shell was a little larger and heavier than both the French 75-mm and all other European or US field guns of the period. This rearmament was completed shortly before the outbreak of World War I. In fact this process of rearmament took place all across Europe, after the continent's military powers had a chance to evaluate the new French gun. As a result, when the great 'war to end all wars' began in August 1914, the field guns and howitzers of the world's leading armies were all roughly similar.

The German Krupp 75-mm field gun, the Austro-Hungarian Skoda 76.5-mm, the Belgian Krupp 75-mm, the Russian Putilov 76.2-mm, the US Ordnance Department 3-inch, and the Japanese Arisaka 75-mm field gun were all minor variants of the ground-breaking French Schneider 75-mm Model 97, and so they all performed their job in the same way. The same was true of howitzers, although here there was more variety. The French favoured a 120-mm barrel, the Germans a 105-mm one, the British a 4.5-inch one (114-mm), while the Russians opted for a 122-mm weapon. Again though, thanks to the lessons learned during the Boer War, the Russo-Japanese War (1904–05) and the more recent wars in the Balkans (1912–13), most countries had embraced similar tactics, and now had the capability to conduct indirect-fire barrages. So, across a continent, armies were now armed with the latest, most modern artillery pieces. It was little wonder that the coming conflict would become known as 'a gunner's war'.

Around the turn of the century, and during the last few years of peace a number of innovations made this new generation of guns even more effective. The gun shield has already been mentioned, this French innovation was adopted by most other countries, even for howitzers which were unlikely to be deployed within small-arms range of the enemy. In fact, changing tactics also rendered this protection less important, at least after the war on the Western Front became a more static affair of trench lines and fixed defensive positions. Similarly, at the start of the war, while horse-drawn gun limbers carried all the ammunition a gun was expected to need, once the war became more static and guns remained in the same position for a long period, this became less useful, and so ammunition was stockpiled beside the guns, brought forward to the batteries by a stream of transport wagons. Eventually, these would be replaced by motorised trucks, and even railways.

While gun carriages became standardised, there were limitations to the arrangement. Usually the lower carriage was a simple affair, as it needed to be easily hitched to a limber and a team of horses. It was the top carriage that was more complicated, as it carried the recoil system, and bore the weight of the gun barrel and gun shield. it was both bulky and heavy, and it had a very limited angle of traverse. This meant that to aim the gun the whole carriage usually needed to be turned by the crew. Designers at the Italian Ansaldo gun factory came up with a novel solution for their 75-mm mountain gun. The trail was split into two legs, which could be spaced widely apart, and therefore improve the arc of fire of the piece. While this notion never really caught on during the war, it was adopted by many countries during the inter-war years.

The big innovation during the first decade of the 20th century was the improvement to gun sights. This in turn had an impact on the ability of the guns to fire at their target, either directly over 'open sights', or by firing at more distant targets using indirect fire. The simple gun sights of the Victorian age – the Gunner's Arc and the Lining Plane – helped a gun crew point their gun at a given mark on the horizon. An observer closer to the target could then work out the bearing from that mark to the target, and tell the gun crew how many degrees to left or right they needed to train their gun. It was hardly a foolproof system, but during the latter part of the Boer War the British used it to pound Boer positions, just as the Japanese did to Russian positions in Manchuria, and the Turks did to their Balkan adversaries. The real development before 1914 was to take this indirect-fire system, and to perfect it using new equipment, and a more sophisticated way of bringing the guns to bear on an unseen target.

The simpler lining plane gave way to a dial sight. Here the gun layer would peer through an eyepiece, and use the device's telescopic sights to identify his mark on the horizon if firing indirectly, or his target if firing 'over open sights'. A built-in scale gave the bearing in degrees, and this could be finely tuned by the gun layer so his crosshairs lay directly over his target. It was reasonably simple to use, and it improved gun accuracy immensely. Essentially though, it was merely a more sophisticated version of earlier sighting gadgets. Its real beauty lay in the ability of all the guns of a gun battery to zero in accurately on the same aiming point. Thanks to the lessons learned during the Boer War, the battery commander would use this system to lay down indirect fire.

The aiming point his battery used would usually be a landmark or an aiming post, staked out between the guns and their target. Other nearby batteries would have their own aiming points, and the distances between these would be calculated, and the angles measured. So, once all this was done, the relative position of all the markers and the gun batteries would be known. From there it was a relatively simple mathematical calculation using a plotting table to give each battery its own set of bearings, so all of the guns would be able to direct their fire on the same unseen target. Eventually the dial sight would be replaced by an indirect fire director, which did the same job, only with greater speed and accuracy. An observation post would direct the fall of shot, and correct the fall of shot by means of flag or lamp signals, or even by radio. Later in the war artillery observations even took to the air, in balloons and aircraft. These developments would be tested on the battlefields of France and Poland, and would prove devastatingly effective.

The guns of August

When the war began in August 1914, nobody really knew what to expect. Certainly all the evidence was there – the deployment of massed artillery batteries, the growing use of machine guns and the ferocity of massed long-range rifle fire, but most people, both soldiers and civilians, still imagined war would be fought in the old way, with gallant bayonet charges, the sweeping use of cavalry, and artillery either stolidly supporting the defenders, or preparing the way for a victorious assault. Few predicted the stultifying effect of machine guns, massed bombardments, trenches, barbed wire and slaughter on a hitherto unimaginable scale.

When the rival armies went to war, they were equipped with artillery designed for a battle of movement, as the Boer War had been, or the Russo-Japanese War, or even the Franco-Prussian War. The first weeks of the war actually happened just like this, a fast-moving fluid campaign fought on both the Eastern and the Western fronts, and in the Balkans. Then the pace of the movement slowed down, at least in the west, and the soldiers began digging in. Soon trench lines stretched from the North Sea coast to the Swiss border, and the fighting became a static form of siege warfare, as both sides tried to break through the enemy's defensive positions. So, the great armies that fought each other to a standstill in 1914 were equipped for the wrong kind of war. Instead of firing at an enemy over 'open sights', the gunners found themselves far behind the front line, pounding the enemy using mass bombardments rather than actually fighting on the battlefield.

One of the opening battles of the war was the siege of Liège, a city the Germans had to capture quickly if they were to march through Belgium and outflank the Anglo-French army. They deployed their powerful siege train, and began bombarding the city's defences on 5 August. The forts surrounding Liège had been rebuilt in the 1890s to withstand bombardment by 200-mm (8-inch) gun – the largest guns of their day. However, the Germans used much larger pieces, including 380-mm siege mortars and a 420-mm siege howitzer nicknamed 'Big Bertha'. One fort exploded when a shell from 'Big Bertha' penetrated a concrete casemate and blew up the fort's magazine. Other forts surrendered when their garrison became trapped in the rubble when their defences were torn apart. The city surrendered after a week of this intense bombardment, and the German army swept on through Belgium towards the English Channel. The siege was a devastating lesson in the effectiveness of modern artillery.

For the next few weeks artillery batteries did indeed fire at the enemy over 'open sights', and often their crews paid the price as their positions were swept by machine-gun and massed rifle fire, or shredded by bursts of shrapnel fired from enemy guns. After the battle of the Marne in September the two sides began digging in, although the German siege guns were soon back in action bombarding the forts protecting Antwerp. An attempt to bypass the Allied line was thwarted around Nieuport on the coast, largely thanks to British naval guns firing in support of the Allied infantry. At one stage their fire was directed by an observer in a balloon, who had a clear view of the enemy lines. Similarly a last-ditch assault on the British lines around

A British 9.2-inch heavy howitzer, dug in on the Western Front, 1916. (Stratford Archive)

Ypres was repelled, the defenders aided by massed gun batteries deployed in defence of the town. It was only on the Eastern Front that the Russians, Germans and Austrians continued to fight a mobile campaign through the winter, and even there, heavy bombardments became more common that dashing actions by individual batteries.

The effectiveness of the German siege guns at Liège was repeated by the Russian guns bombarding the Austro-Hungarian fortress city of Lemberg (Lvov). The effectiveness of large siege howitzers at bombarding Belgian and Austrian forts demonstrated that static defences were ill-prepared to withstand a bombardment from the immense shells used against them. The only limitation to their use was the difficulty of transporting these immense guns. At Antwerp, 'Big Bertha' was too large and cumbersome to easily transport using horse limbers. Instead, it needed a railway line nearby to bring the dismantled gun and its ammunition and equipment to the siege lines. With a range of over 15,000 metres it could comfortably sit behind the lines, safe from enemy counter-battery fire. The Austrian Skoda 305-mm siege howitzers were almost as effective and so other nations, who had hitherto limited the size of the guns in their siege trains, began to consider developing monster guns of their own.

The British had already been developing a 9.2-inch siege howitzer, and in late 1914 it was rushed into production. An even larger 15-inch version was developed too – effectively a scaled-up version of the 9.2-inch, but the effectiveness of both howitzers was limited by their relatively paltry range of 10,000 yards. By 1917 both the British and the Germans had withdrawn their super-howitzers from front-line service, as they were out-ranged by a new generation of improved field howitzers.

More successful was the railway gun. These weapons were essentially large siege howitzers which were mounted on railway carriages. This meant that weight and transport wasn't a serious issue, and if the guns came under enemy counter-battery fire they could be moved out of the way with relative ease. Before the war the French had rejected the establishment of a powerful siege train – instead they preferred to rely on their far more mobile field guns. However, the lessons learned from Liege and the fighting around Verdun led to the development of heavy guns, and the deployment of coastal guns as makeshift siege weapons. Meanwhile the Schneider gun factory developed their own 520-mm (20-inch) siege howitzer which they dubbed a 'fort buster'. It was mounted on a railway wagon, but of the two guns made, one burst during trials, and the other never saw action.

Undeterred, the United States had developed their large guns for coastal defence, and when the country belatedly entered the war in 1917 some of these weapons were converted into railway guns. These were mainly 8-inch pieces, although only three of them reached France before the end of the war. By then the need for such guns had largely evaporated. The attempts to break the deadlock of trench warfare meant that from 1915 on, both sides made greater use of medium-sized guns – weapons with the range and versatility to play a decisive part in the great offensives which characterised this phase of the war.

The powerful French Rimailho 155-mm howitzer introduced in 1904 was one of the oldest of these, with a fairly modest range of 6,600 yards. While the German Krupp 105-mm howitzer which entered production five years later had a similar range, later wartime variants firing more modern ammunition extended this to over 11,00 yards. This compared well with the British Vickers 4.5-inch howitzer which had a 7,000-yard range, the Austro-Hungarian 104-mm Model 1899 howitzer (6,500 yards) or the Russian Putilov 122-mm howitzer with its maximum range of 7,300 yards. For all their minor differences all these guns did essentially the same job – using indirect fire they would pound the enemy trenches, often in bombardments lasting several hours, destroying the defences, and wearing down the enemy's morale. Given the nature of trench warfare, these howitzers proved far more useful than field guns.

This reflects the changing nature of artillery tactics. When the war began, field guns were meant to fulfil the traditional artillery function of supporting the infantry line using direct fire, either in offensive operations or in defence. When mobile campaigning gave way to trench warfare this role was abandoned, and the field gun batteries in all armies were used to provide indirect fire. They were less suited to this than howitzer batteries, but most gunners were well versed in modern indirect-fire techniques, and at the very least the field guns were able to lend their weight to bombardments. This – the use of large-scale bombardment – remained the principal role of artillery throughout the war. The other useful task, conducting counter-battery fire, was a specialist role, which became more important as the war progressed.

At first, barrages were simply that – all the guns would fire at the target for a prescribed length of time, or a set number of rounds. Shells would be stockpiled before the bombardment, and the fire would be conducted according to a pre-arranged fire plan, where each gun or battery would fire on its prescribed bearing and elevation. By 1915 the rolling barrage had developed as a useful variant. In this, the battery would fire at a certain point, and then at a pre-arranged rate it would 'walk' its fire forward along a set path, heading towards the enemy lines. This allowed infantry assaults to follow immediately behind a rolling barrage as it crept forward, which in theory prevented the enemy from re-manning their defences before the infantrymen reached the enemy trench line. The only counter the enemy had to this was to dig deeper, and to reinforce their front-line bunkers.

A later variant was the box barrage, where the guns would surround an area with a curtain of fire, preventing reinforcements from reaching the enemy trenches in the middle of the box. A protective barrage was similar, only it was designed to keep the enemy from crossing these 'beaten zones', so preventing them from launching an attack. A variant of this was to forestall enemy assaults by firing a counter-preparation barrage, targeting potential enemy assembly points or rear areas. Finally, counter-battery fire required an observer to detect the enemy battery, map its location, and then to bring down fire on the battery's position. As the war progressed counter-battery missions became increasingly sophisticated, with aerial reconnaissance, listening posts, and the use of triangulation to pinpoint the location of hidden enemy batteries. While the conflict might have been a gunner's war, artillery batteries close to the front line were consequently almost as vulnerable to enemy fire as the infantrymen in the front-line trenches.

The big gun battleship

While the two decades from 1860 until 1880 had seen a phenomenal degree of change in warship design, the last two decades of the century saw this pace slow, allowing a more gradual naval evolution to take place. Regardless of where they were built, all of the major battleships of this period were broadly similar to each other. They carried four big guns, mounted in two twin turrets, at the bow and the stern of the ship. In between lay a battery of secondary guns – usually 4- to 6-inch pieces, with smaller quick-firing guns offering these ships some protection against small, fast-moving torpedo boats. These battleships were only tested in battle a few times during this period – in the Sino-Japanese War (1894–95), the Spanish-American War (1898) and the Russo-Japanese War (1904–05).

The guns used in these ships were large breech-loading weapons, such as the 12-inch guns of British manufacture carried in Japanese battleships, or the similar-sized guns made in Russia to a French design, carried in the more modern Russian capital ships. That the naval campaigns of these three wars all proved decisive owed far more to strategy than to tactics, and with all ships broadly the same in terms of capabilities, the advantage lay with those ships whose crew was better trained or had higher morale than their opponents. At the time Britain had the largest navy in the world – larger than the combined navies of any two of its potential rivals. In theory this meant that it was in Britain's interests to maintain this naval status quo. However, when faced with disquieting rumours of more advanced ships being built abroad, Admiral of the Fleet Sir John 'Jackie' Fisher decided that Britain needed to build these advanced ships before her rivals. So, the era of the 'big gun battleship' was born.

Fisher believed that rather than equip a battleship with two pairs of large guns and a battery of lighter pieces, it should only carry big guns – as many as it could carry. Similarly this new 'all big gun battleship' should be protected by armour thick enough to deflect enemy big guns. Fisher had his naval architects design just such a vessel, which was laid down in October 1905. Just four months later, in February 1906, she was launched as HMS *Dreadnought*, a ship which revolutionised the naval world. *Dreadnought* carried ten 12-inch guns in five twin turrets, although due to her configuration a maximum of only eight guns could bear on a target at any one time. She was protected by a steel belt up to 11 inches thick, and powered by turbine engines which gave her an impressive top speed of

The 13.5-inch forward guns of the dreadnought King George V, *pictured in 1918. (Stratford Archive)*

21 knots. Essentially, *Dreadnought* immediately rendered all existing battleships obsolete. She could take on a whole squadron of them and still expect to win. Soon, existing battleships were given the disparaging term of 'pre-dreadnoughts'.

More 'dreadnoughts' would follow, as this ground-breaking warship lent her name to a whole new class of warship. The appearance of *Dreadnought* ushered in an Anglo-German naval arms race that heightened international tension, and arguably led indirectly to the outbreak of the world war. Not only Britain and Germans built dreadnoughts and lighter battlecruisers (fast dreadnoughts without the armour) – France, Italy, Russia, the USA, Japan and a couple of South American countries built dreadnoughts too, during the last years of peace. The dreadnought was armed with 12-inch breech-loading guns designed by Vickers. While these were no different from the guns fitted to the more modern pre-dreadnoughts, what set *Dreadnought* and her successors apart was their fire control system. In theory, these 12-inch guns had a maximum range of up to 24,000 yards, but the pre-dreadnought battleship lacked the fire control systems fitted to dreadnoughts, and so battles were normally fought at ranges of 8,000 yards or less. In other words, the guns weren't achieving their full potential.

The fire control system in dreadnoughts consisted of three main elements – an observer, a calculating machine, and the guns themselves. The observer or gunnery director used powerful optical rangefinders to work out the range and bearing of the target. This information was fed into a mechanical calculating machine, or rather a group of machines, which combined this tracking information with other data – the wind speed and direction, the course and speed of both ships, weather conditions and the rate the range was opening or closing. These calculators plotted all this, and the result of their calculation was sent to the gun turrets in the form of the nearing and elevation the guns needed to be at in order to hit the target. Once all the guns were trained on the enemy the whole salvo would be fired simultaneously using electrical signals.

Ideally the salvo would hit the target. If not the observers would report the error – usually an overshoot or undershoot, and the range would be corrected. It was a complex system – much more so than the methods used to plot the fall of shot on land – but it was extremely effective. Once on target these guns could then pound the enemy ship at a rate of one full salvo every 40 seconds. The combined destructive power of these salvos was phenomenal. At the battle of Jutland (1916) whole ships blew up when hit by salvos of enemy shells. It just took one shell to penetrate the target's armour and explode, thereby setting off an internal magazine explosion from powder charges in the turret and a flash blast down to the magazine to rip a ship apart. At Jutland the majority of German dreadnoughts and battlecruisers were fitted with 11-inch or 12-inch guns, while the British used 12-inch, 13.5-inch, 14-inch and even 15-inch guns. A squadron of four modern dreadnoughts therefore carried more destructive power than hundreds of land-based field guns and howitzers. Naval warfare had become a clash of huge steel titans, armed with the most powerful artillery pieces in history.

Ironically, these guns rarely fired in anger. Jutland was the only full-scale naval battle of the war, and while technically it was a draw, the German High Seas Fleet was outmanoeuvred and lucky to escape. They made two sorties after Jutland, and each time the German fleet avoided battle, as their fleet was outgunned and outnumbered. So, Britain was able to maintain its devastatingly effective naval blockade of Germany. Ultimately this led to Germany's surrender in 1918, achieving through starvation what the generals had failed to achieve on land. Jutland was also a salutary lesson in what not to do. On dreadnoughts, shells and ammunition bags were brought up from the magazines to the gun turrets using electro-mechanical hoists. Blast-proof doors were meant to prevent a hit on the turret resulting in a flash fire which would race down the hoists into the magazines. At Jutland some of these doors were left open to increase the speed of loading – four British ships and their crews paid the ultimate price for placing speed over safety. The same mistake wasn't made again.

Late war innovations

The demands of the war took both generals and arms manufacturers by surprise. Before August 1914 nobody could have predicted just how many shells would be needed. It was later calculated that during the first months of the war German guns averaged a thousand rounds per day – more than half the expected barrel life of the gun. Once trench warfare began and massed barrages became commonplace the demand for ammunition became even greater. On every front ammunition stocks were husbanded while more shells could be mass-produced, and in 1915 this supply and demand problem developed into a full-scale ammunition crisis. Eventually the crisis was solved in Britain by diverting industrial resources to shell production and the replacement of worn-out gun barrels. The Germans and the

French lacked the industrial capacity to do this so effectively, and so for them the crisis never completely went away, although the French eventually benefited from American industrial output during the last year of the war.

While most wartime guns were merely replacements for existing models, or at best minor variants of them, designers managed to dramatically improve the performance of these weapons. For example, in 1914 the British 18-pounder had a range of 6,500 yards, but by 1918 this had increased to 9,300 yards, as a new carriage design permitted greater elevation. Ammunition was improved too, both in terms of its effectiveness and its reliability. The first gas shells were developed by the Germans, and used on the Eastern Front in January 1915. These proved ineffective, but by the end of the year more reliable gas shells for howitzers were in service on the Western Front. Other warring nations produced their own versions, but gas shells were used sparingly during the war, as they proved relatively ineffective compared to other forms of ammunition. In fact, a German bombardment of mustard gas shells came to be used as a defensive measure, as it lingered, and effectively prevented anyone from moving through the area for several days.

A far more innovative development was the increased use of mechanisation to move artillery around the battlefield. One of the problems with artillery pieces of this period was their inability to follow up an advance. Before a major offensive the enemy line would be bombarded for several days, and this churned up the ground. Rain then made it a sea of mud, which was largely impassable to horse-drawn artillery limbers. So, if the attack was successful, the relatively short range of the guns meant that the infantry would soon move beyond the range of their supporting guns. A way had to be found to move the guns across the shell-scarred terrain.

For larger guns the solution was the laying of narrow gauge railway tracks. Then, the guns and their ammunition could be moved forward, although the pace of the advance was limited by the ability to lay track. Traction engines were also used, although their weight limited their effectiveness as artillery tows. Behind the lines, motorised vehicles were adapted to either carry guns on their backs, or else be used as towing vehicles, effectively replacing horse and limber teams. These were seen in greater numbers during the last years of the war, but essentially the bulk of artillery remained horse-drawn. The tank was invented largely to provide support for infantry during an advance. Although these only carried light field pieces or machine guns, they certainly proved effective, and by the end of the war most of the leading military powers – Britain, France, Germany and the USA – had developed their own tracked fighting vehicles. While they might have represented the future of warfare, these early tanks still lacked the reliability and performance to make a major difference on the battlefield.

In 1917 the French went one stage further and adapted a tracked chassis to carry an artillery piece. Both the Schneider and St. Chamond arms factories produced their own pioneering versions of these tracked artillery transports, but these remained experimental, and their poor performance meant that they were never able to take to the field. Still, it was an innovative solution to the problem of transporting guns across a shell-ravaged battlefield, and while the vehicles themselves might not have been particularly effective, the idea was clearly a sound one, and would form the basis for what today is a standard battlefield weapon – the self-propelled gun. Another by-product of the tank was the development of anti-tank guns. While most field guns could destroy the lightly armed and slow-moving tanks of this period, their deployment led to the development of specialist anti-tank guns, usually small high-velocity quick-firing weapons.

Another reaction to changing circumstances was the creation of the anti-aircraft gun. The use of observation balloons during the 19th century had led to spasmodic attempt to convert ordnance to shoot them down. Experiments in France and Britain began in 1910–11, but it was Germany who led the way, developing effective anti-balloon guns as early as 1909. However, it was the wartime development of the aeroplane that created an urgent need for such weapons. These were relatively fast-moving, and so an anti-aircraft gun had to be able to track the aircraft as it flew past. Machine guns were easily adapted into light anti-aircraft weapons, as were light quick-firing guns fitted to pedestal-style mounts. From 1914 larger guns of 75-mm (3-inch) calibre were deployed by Britain, France, Germany and Austria-Hungary as anti-aircraft weapons, using shrapnel shells fitted with timers, so they would burst in the air. These shells were later adapted so they would explode when they reached a set altitude. This permitted the firing of anti-aircraft (or 'flak') barrage, sending up a wall of shrapnel in front of an aircraft. Again, this was a weapon whose real heyday lay in the future. For now though, anti-aircraft guns provided an effective counter to the slow-moving and frail aircraft of the period.

By the end of this gruelling conflict in November 1918 the artilleryman's world had changed for ever. When the war began, guns were largely seen as a means of offering close fire support to infantry and cavalry on the battlefield. Four years later they had become the key element in modern warfare, capable of unleashing a devastating level of firepower on the enemy through mass bombardment. Guns were used for purposes that didn't exist in 1914, and wartime advances in the field of indirect fire meant that they were far more deadly than they had ever been before. Many experts thought that by 1918 artillery had reached a plateau of development, and while minor improvements might be made, the artillery piece had reached the limit of its development. Few predicted that in just over two decades, artillery would once again be pushing the boundaries of its development, as a new generation of guns would be tested in a new and even more challenging global conflict.

CHAPTER 7

WORLD WAR II AND AFTER

1919–present

WORLD WAR I MIGHT HAVE BEEN 'a gunner's war', but it was fought using outdated equipment, designed for a very different kind of conflict. This meant that when it ended almost all the combatants had large stocks of outmoded artillery pieces on their hands. The exception was Germany, which was demilitarised when the war ended. At other times this might have prompted a redesign of artillery to reflect wartime developments. Instead, the conflict was dubbed 'the war to end all wars', and military expenditure was cut back. After all, if there would be no more large-scale wars, what need was there for expensive artillery pieces? Still, while development took place, it happened very slowly. However, the war created the need for new types of guns such as anti-aircraft and anti-tank weapons. As development of both tanks and aircraft continued during the inter-war period, so too did the search for guns to counter these new threats.

The inter-war years

In 1918, the US War Department began an investigation into the US Army's artillery, and the lessons that could be learned from the war. Thus the United States was the first country to properly evaluate its artillery, and to look at its future. This led to the scrapping of obsolete guns, and the consolidation of the American artillery park into just four models of guns. The investigative board recommended further research into projectiles, motor transport and the development of self-propelled guns. America's lead was followed by other countries – both Britain and France conducted a similar type of review, although they came up with very different solutions. The French felt there was nothing wrong with their classic 75-mm field gun of 1897 – all it needed were a few modifications, which were duly made in 1922. This increased the gun's range, and a variant introduced in 1933 replaced its carriage with a more flexible split-trail version, but essentially the gun was outdated in 1918, and by 1939 it was completely obsolete.

In Britain it was clear the existing field guns needed to be replaced, as did the 4.5-inch howitzer. The problem was, nobody seemed to agree what to replace them with. It was eventually decided to opt for one gun to replace all three weapons, and after much deliberation the 25-pounder gun-howitzer was selected. In the meantime the 18-pounder remained in service, but was re-bored and fitted with a new rifled sleeve to take a larger 25-pounder shell. The carriage wasn't strong enough to take the full force of the modified gun's recoil, and so reduced charges were used until proper 25-pounders finally appeared. The new 25-pounder finally entered service in 1935–36, the gun mounted on a box trail carriage that sat on its own turntable. This proved an ingenious design, as it made the gun extremely easy to train, and gave it a 360° traverse. The 25-pounder had a maximum range of 13,400 yards, and proved to be one of the artillery success stories of the war.

Between the wars a large proportion of Britain's limited military budget was spent building up the coastal defences of Singapore, and the United States did the same in Manila Harbour in the Philippines. Enormous naval-sized guns were emplaced in these

A 25-pounder in action, Western Desert, 1941. (Stratford Archive)

positions, but when war came to both places in 1941 these coastal defences meekly surrendered, as the Japanese captured Singapore and Manila from the land, rather than by amphibious assault. Even more impressive was the Maginot Line, a thick belt of fortified outposts guarding France's border with Germany. Artillery pieces were mounted in ingenious armoured cupolas, or placed to create killing grounds in front of fortified bunkers, while underground railways linked the guns to their magazines. In 1940, the Germans simply bypassed the Maginot Line by advancing through Belgium instead. So, these fortifications proved to be a waste of money.

Germany had been largely disarmed after the war, and restrictions placed on the type of artillery Germany could have. This also meant that there was no stock of older guns, meaning German designers were free to create modern artillery pieces. Krupp sent staff to work with other manufacturers abroad, and gradually new designs evolved, drawing on the latest principles. As a result, when Nazi Germany began openly re-arming its military forces in 1933, the German army began receiving modern and well-designed ordnance. By 1940 the army could field over 50,000 mortars and artillery pieces, and that summer

A German 105mm leFH 18 howitzer in action, Russia, 1942. (Stratford Archive)

these were used with devastating effectiveness during the campaign against France and the Low Countries.

As the war clouds loomed the potential rivals made the final selection of the guns that would serve them during the coming war. While the French retained their 75-mm field gun, in 1935 they also introduced a new 105-mm howitzer mounted on a split trail carriage. It was very similar to the German 105-mm Model 1919 light field howitzer, which was designed in 1929–30, but only entered service in 1935. Like the French the Germans retained a 75-mm field gun, which they used as a light infantry support weapon.

This German howitzer had a respectable range of 11,650 yards, and with some modifications it proved a reliable gun throughout the war. The Italians fielded the 75-mm Model 11 field gun that had served them well during the previous war. Still, it was the first artillery piece to be mounted on a split trail carriage, and while it was old, it remained in service until Italy's surrender in 1943.

The Japanese lagged behind the Europeans in terms of gun design, and so when they entered the war their main field gun was a 75-mm Type 38 based on a Krupp design first produced in 1905. It was modified slightly though, and given a new trail which earned it the designation 'Type 38 Improved', but it was still an outdated gun. In 1930 a 75-mm Type 90 appeared, based on an old Schneider design, but it proved even less effective than its predecessor. The US Army stuck with its 75-mm field gun and the 105-mm and 155-mm howitzers it had retained in 1918. By 1941 the modified versions of these guns were more effective than their predecessors. The new 75-mm field gun M2A2 was an effective weapon, but it was gradually replaced by the more useful 105-mm field howitzer M2A1. Thousands of these guns saw service during the war, and it proved an extremely reliable and versatile weapon.

During the late 1920s the Soviet Union began a major rearmament, which saw the development of several excellent artillery pieces. By 1941 the 76.2-mm field gun M39/42 was in service, with its split trail carriage. An anti-tank version of the same weapon was also produced, which gave these guns a dual role. Similarly the old 122-mm field howitzer was replaced by the M38 model, an altogether modern weapon which remained in widespread use until the 1960s. Again, an anti-tank version labelled the 122-mm D30 was eventually produced. The remodelled Soviet Army placed a great emphasis on its artillery arm, and so these new guns were manufactured in great numbers – over 67,000 were in service by 1941. As a result, after it recovered from the initial German invasion of Russia, these Russian guns would play a significant part in the counter-offensive that ultimately led to the fall of Berlin.

Wartime developments

The 'phoney war' from September 1939 to May 1940 might have eased the transition from peace to war, but it did little to test the effectiveness of artillery. It was only when the Germans unleashed their *blitzkrieg* against France and her allies that the faults were exposed. Sometimes these were minor. For instance, in Britain an artillery regiment was incorporated into an infantry division, and charged with supporting a brigade of infantry. However, the brigade had three battalions, but the artillery regiment only had two 12-gun batteries. The solution to restructure the regiment into three 8-gun batteries was only put into effect after the debacle in France. By that time the bulk of the British army and a sizeable portion of the French had been evacuated from Dunkirk, but while the troops escaped, their artillery was left behind.

The French field gun proved ineffective compared to the latest German guns, while the speed of the German advance owed much to its reliance on trucks. This said, while the panzer formations were supported by fully motorised infantry, those serving the German infantry divisions were still largely horse-drawn. So, while the infantry divisions advanced slowly, the panzer formations raced across Belgium and Northern France, and cut the Allied armies in two. During this *blitzkrieg* the motorised artillery were able to keep pace with the panzers, and so were able to use their firepower whenever the German spearhead encountered resistance. These panzer formations were also supported by a small number of self-propelled assault guns, an excellent solution to the problem of providing close artillery support to fast-moving columns of tanks and mechanised troops. These lessons were not lost on the Allies.

During the inter-war years there had been some resistance to the replacement of horse-drawn limbers with mechanised gun tractors (or tows), but the increased reliability of vehicles and the development of half-tracked artillery tows helped convince sceptics. Still, horse-drawn units remained in use for much of the war, even in the German army. The French, who had fielded the world's first mechanised artillery regiment before World War I, were particularly reliant on horses during the 1940 campaign. Eventually though, horse-drawn limbers became the exception. They were done away with entirely in the highly mechanised British and American armies of the latter half of the war. In the German army, fuel shortages led to a resurgence in the use of horse-drawn limbers during the last years of the war, and in Normandy thousands of artillery and ammunition draught-horses were killed in the fighting.

The self-propelled gun was also a development first pioneered by the French during World War I, when they built motorised anti-aircraft weapons. The Italians followed the French lead, but it was the British who were the first to use a fully tracked chassis to propel an artillery piece. This 'gun carrying tank' underwent trials in early 1917, but it never entered service during the war. Similarly the French developed their own experimental self-propelled 220-mm howitzer, but it never went into production. During the 1920s, American, British and French designers continued to develop self-propelled weapons, but none appeared before the outbreak of war. Instead the British persisted with portees – essentially guns mounted on the back of trucks, and portee anti-tank guns saw action in the Western Desert.

During 1939–40, the Germans began mounting artillery pieces on tank chassis to support their infantry – the Sturmgeschütz III developed during the late 1930s carried a 75-mm gun, and first proved its worth during the Fall of France (1940). While it was later adapted to become a tank-hunter, other German self-propelled infantry guns, such as the SiG 33 self-propelled gun mounting a 150-mm infantry gun, remained pure assault guns. Later, in 1943, the Wespe entered service as a fully fledged self-propelled gun, combining a 105-mm howitzer with the chassis of a Panzer II tank. It was followed by the Hummel, which carried a 155-mm howitzer. These vehicles were eventually grouped into self-propelled artillery battalions attached to panzer divisions. In addition, the Germans made good use of the guns and vehicles they captured to produce a range of self-propelled vehicles, created to augment their mobile forces.

In the Allied camp it was the Americans who produced the first self-propelled guns, mounted on half-tracks and used as tank destroyers. This though, was followed in 1943 by the M7 Priest, which combined the chassis of a Sherman tank with a 105-mm howitzer. It was produced in significant numbers during the war, and proved an excellent vehicle. The British equivalent was the Sexton, which was also introduced in 1943, and married the same Sherman chassis with a 25-pounder gun-howitzer. However, it was the Soviet Union who really made the greatest use of the self-propelled gun during the war.

From the 1920s the Soviet Union had been experimenting with the mounting of anti-tank guns and infantry guns on tracked chassis. In late 1942 Soviet designers produced the SU-76, a small self-propelled gun mounting a 76-mm gun on a light tank chassis. It was an anti-tank weapon, but the similarly designed SU-122 carried a 122-mm howitzer, and proved to be one of the most effective and assault gun designs of the war, as well as the most numerous. It was followed in early 1943 by the SU-152, a massively armoured beast of a self-propelled gun that, like its lighter predecessor, was specifically designed to be used in a close support role. These though weren't self-propelled guns in the purest sense – they were direct-fire weapons, and their guns used to pound enemy strongpoints rather than to lay down indirect fire. For that the Russians preferred their conventional artillery, which by 1944–45 had reached such numbers that for major offensives like the drive on Berlin, concentrations of 200–300 guns and howitzers for every thousand yards of front line were the sledgehammer the Russians used to smash the German army.

Specialist ordnance

The war was very different from the previous global conflict. For the most part it was far more mobile, particularly on the Eastern Front, and in North Africa. Trench warfare was largely avoided, which meant there was less need for siege artillery – heavy guns whose main aim was to pound the enemy's defences, or destroy his own artillery concentrations. Large howitzers still continued to be used, as did large railway guns and other super-heavy pieces of ordnance, but these were no longer viewed as the wonder weapons their counterparts were seen as a quarter of a century before. Still, the Germans designed the 800-mm railway guns *Gustav* and *Dora* specifically to pound the defences of the French Maginot Line. They were never needed, and in fact only *Gustav* saw action, bombarding Sevastopol in 1942, and Warsaw two years later. Sixty trains were needed to bring the gun to the front line and as the German commander at Sevastopol noted, its military value wasn't worth the effort taken to build it and bring it into action.

More effective were the large siege guns the Germans deployed near Calais to fire across the English Channel at Dover. The guns continued their intermittent shelling of the English port until their batteries were overrun in September 1944. While devastating to the townspeople of Dover, it was little more than a propaganda exercise. The military value of these guns was minimal. Far more useful were the large howitzers used by most major armies during the war. These included the British 4.5-inch, and its more effective 5.5-inch counterpart, the German 150-mm sFH18 howitzer, the Soviet 122-mm M30 and 152-mm M10 howitzers, the US 155-mm M-1 howitzer, and the Italian 149.1-mm Model 1937 howitzer. All of these large and powerful guns had a range of around 10,000–12,000 yards, although later in the war the range of some Allied guns was extended thanks to improved propellants and projectiles. These guns were all so large that separate shells and powder charges were required, but then rate of fire was considered less important than range and accuracy.

The mortar had effectively been relegated as a weapon in the later 19th century, when the first modern howitzers appeared. It was resurrected as an infantry support weapon in 1915 following the introduction of the 3-inch Stokes trench mortar, a light and portable short-range mortar designed to target enemy trenches. The Germans responded with their own trench mortar, the Granatwerfer, and while these never saw widespread service beyond the Western Front, the value of an infantry mortar was recognised, and by World War II it had become a standard weapon in most modern armies. By then, these mortars used streamlined fin-stabilised projectiles (or 'bombs'), that were more accurate and had an enhanced range. Typically, an infantry mortar of World War II had a range of around 2,500 yards, and a well-trained mortar crew could fire 20–30 rounds per minute.

Several kinds of mortars existed, from the small 2-inch or 50-mm mortars used primarily to fire smoke projectiles to a new breed of heavy such as the German and Soviet 120-mm and the British 4.2-inch mortars. While standard mortars of 75–85-mm calibre were really regarded as infantrymen's weapons, and were allocated in small sections to infantry formations, these heavier mortars were usually grouped in larger batteries, and operated as fully fledged indirect-fire artillery weapons. Interestingly, both in the Germans and the US armies, half-tracks were used to provide additional mobility to mortars when attached to armoured formations. The Soviets made particular use of these heavy mortars, deploying whole regiments of them to augment their already formidable artillery forces.

A new weapon related to the mortar was the rocket. In China, rockets had been used on the battlefield as early as the 11th century, and in India during the 17th and 18th centuries, but their use in Europe had a much shorter pedigree. During the French Revolutionary War Sir William Congreve developed experimental rockets which he described as 'ammunition without ordnance'. These Congreve rockets were used during naval attacks on Boulogne and Copenhagen, and rocket batteries were tried out on land, most notably at the battle of Leipzig (1813), but their performance was too erratic for accurate use on the battlefield. These early war rockets looked remarkably like modern sky rockets, and were used the same way, the sticks attached to the warhead being inserted into a firing tube before the fuse was lit. Experiments with rockets continued throughout the 19th century, by which time rockets resembled artillery shells, and were fired from small steel troughs. However, by the later 19th century these weapons were rarely used.

During World War I both the British and the Germans experimented with rockets, but neither country produced a rocket worthy of being used on the battlefield. In 1930 the Germans resumed their work on rocketry, and by 1933 they produced rockets capable of firing indirectly at distant targets. By 1940 these had evolved into the A4 (known to the Allies as the V2), which was almost 50 feet long, and had a range of approximately 200 miles. This was used as a long-distance terror weapon, pounding London from rocket sites on the far side of the English Channel. For their part the British developed a small rocket as an anti-aircraft weapon, designed to be launched in large batches, with each rocket trailing a wire. The idea was to place a lethal obstacle in the path of enemy bombers.

Then, in 1939, the Germans produced a rocket system designed for use on the battlefield. They called it the 'Nebelwerfer' (smoke mortar), as it was originally designed to fire gas or smoke shells as well as regular high-explosive ordnance. The main production version had a calibre of 150mm, and had six barrels. Each fired a fin-stabilised projectile that resembled a large mortar bomb, and while its maximum range of around 2,500 yards was moderate, when firing high-explosive projectiles the Nebelwerfer proved devastatingly effective. The Allies dubbed it the 'Moaning Minnie', due to the curious sound these projectiles made while in flight. Later in the war the Germans produced larger-calibre versions, albeit in smaller numbers, and these proved equally effective.

Meanwhile the Soviet Union had been developing their own 'rocket-powered shells' throughout the 1930s, and by 1939 they had produced a 132-mm rocket system, grouped in batteries of 24 rockets and rail launchers, and designed to be fired virtually simultaneously from the back of a truck. The weapon had a range of around 9,500 yards and, while far less accurate than a conventional artillery bombardment, these rockets were designed as saturation weapons, plastering the target with high explosives. The Russians nicknamed their new weapon the 'Katyusha', while the Germans, who grew to fear them, calling them 'Stalin's Organs'.

While only 40 Katyusha trucks were in service in the summer of 1941, they were mass-produced during the war, and by 1945 over 2,000 of these weapons were in front-line service. Again, improved versions were produced as the war progressed, and rail-mounted versions were also developed. The Western Allies used a variant of this system to bombard the German defences on D-Day, and during other amphibious operations, but their use remained limited.

Projectiles and propellants

During the war the need to mass-produce artillery pieces meant there was a reluctance to develop new types of artillery. A much more efficient use of industrial resources was to improve the performance of the gun types already in service. One obvious way to extend range was to improve the gun's propellant. The nitrocellulose propellant developed by the US Army during the war proved erratic due to its susceptability to damp, but late in the war a more stable nitrogen-enriched British alternative appeared which combined nitrocellulose, nitroglycerine and picrite. Both of these new propellants improved the range of a projectile by around 10 per cent, as did similar German nitrocellulose-based explosives. However, this was hardly a major improvement in performance.

A more promising avenue was the idea of redesigning the projectile itself. Tungsten carbide was twice as stiff as steel and so, despite its scarcity, it became a favoured metal for use in armour-piercing rounds, which had to force their way through steel obstacles such as the armoured belt of ships, tanks or fortifications. Due to wartime shortages the Germans abandoned the use of tungsten in 1942, and the British found the performance of tungsten-core shells was less impressive than they'd hoped for. However, development in the United States continued, and 'composite rigid' shells containing a tungsten core wrapped in a steel casing eventually proved to be efficient enough to produce as anti-tank rounds.

The development of the sabot shell was even more effective. During the 1930s the French pioneered the use of firing a shell wrapped in a sabot or sleeve, which gave the projectile a greater velocity than a regular shell of the same calibre. Once fired the sabot would fall away from the shell, which would continue its high-velocity flight towards its target. The Germans followed the French lead and began developing sabot rounds of their own, particularly for use in anti-tank guns, where a higher velocity meant a better penetration of the enemy tank's armour. While the Americans persisted with their 'composite rigid' shells to give them better penetration, the British also adopted the sabot system, and by 1944 the APDS (armour-piercing discarding sabot) round had entered general service as an anti-tank projectile.

The high explosive anti-tank (HEAT) round was another form of projectile developed during the 1930s, this time in Switzerland, but during the war it was largely used as an anti-tank round used in portable infantry weapons, such as the German panzerfaust or the American bazooka. This was a form of shallow charge (or shaped charge). The idea behind it was that a cavity in the head of a shell would improve the penetrative power of the projectile. It was lined with a metal such as copper that, when the charge detonated, would form a jet of molten metal and gas that could penetrate armour. While used for infantry support weapons, it was also useful for artillery pieces. This shaped charge round effectively gave wartime field guns and howitzers an anti-tank capability, so in an emergency they could defend their battery position by engaging the approaching tanks over 'open sights'. On several occasions British 25-pounders had to do just that during the war in the desert.

Countering new threats

Artillery was the undoubted 'queen of the battlefield' during World War I. However, two new rivals emerged during the war, and while their development of aircraft and tanks were still in their infancy, they would soon threaten the supremacy of artillery on the battlefield. By 1917 the aircraft had already evolved into an efficient war machine that could strike artillery positions far behind the front line, while tanks, if properly handled, could overrun enemy trench lines and break out into the enemy's rear where his artillery batteries were sited. The development of both aircraft and tanks proved rapid during the inter-war years, so that by 1939 they could potentially dominate the modern battlefield. In German hands, a combination of the two provided the cornerstones of the *blitzkrieg* that proved so devastatingly successful in 1940.

In most countries between 1919 and 1939 the development of effective anti-aircraft (AA) guns lagged behind the development of combat aircraft. Still, the growing threat posed by aircraft was understood, and so during the 1930s the production of AA guns would become more of a priority. Much as they had done in World War I, AA guns fell into two groups. Light anti-aircraft guns relied on a high volume of fire to bring down an aircraft, while larger weapons achieved the same time by putting up a flak barrage, designed to do the same by using air bursting shells. While the aircraft of the previous conflict had a very limited ceiling, and guns rarely needed to reach targets above 10,000 feet, aircraft in service were now flying at over 30,000 feet, and so heavy flak guns had to hit targets at a greater height than before.

In most countries, heavy anti-aircraft guns were quick-firing weapons with a bore size of over 75 mm (3 inches), and capable of high-angle fire, meaning they could elevate almost vertically. Examples of guns of this type include the British 3.7-inch and the German 88-mm Flak 36, which also proved to be a superb anti-tank gun too.

Light AA guns were either single- or multi-barrelled weapons, with a calibre of 20–40mm. Typically they were magazine-fed to increase their rate of fire. The German relied on quadruple-barrelled 20-mm guns and single-barrelled 37-mm weapons, while the western Allies also used 20-mm weapons, usually manufactured by Oerlikon. The superb 40-mm Bofors gun was increasingly used, while the British also employed the older 2-pounder (40-mm) 'Pom-Pom', based on a quick-firing gun first developed during the Boer War. The Soviets used a 37-mm gun, which was essentially their own version of the Bofors. At sea the same lack of preparation during the 1930s meant that at the start of the war many ships were unable to offer an adequate defence against attacking aircraft. Machine-gun AA guns proved too ineffective and short-ranged to deal with modern aircraft, and so the solution was to mount multiple light AA guns, while also developing larger high-angle guns capable of adding to the ship's defence. For many warships, these developments came too late to protect them from attack.

The real development during the war was the introduction of fire control systems capable of accurately predicting when an air attack would take place, allowing the defender to effectively target the enemy planes. The British developed an effective radar

The powerful battleship HMS Rodney *carried both radar and a battery of AA guns. (Stratford Archive)*

system in 1940, which was then shared with the United States. This, combined with accurate fire control systems in warships and in ground-based AA batteries permitted the accurate deployment of flak barrages designed to stop enemy aircraft. Eventually, radar-controlled gunfire became possible, and this proved particularly effective at sea. Short-range protection remained the preserve of light AA guns, where volume of fire was the key. On the battlefield, the use of fast fighter-bombers meant that all the warring powers needed to provide adequate AA protection for their troops. This led to the proliferation of light AA guns, while heavier guns were used to protect cities from enemy bombers, particularly in Britain, 1940–44, and Germany, 1943–45. Again, fire control and early warning systems proved vital in allowing guns to counter the threat posed by aircraft, rather than any technological development of the guns themselves.

The development of radar also had a dramatic impact on naval warfare. During the inter-war years there was little change in the size or capability of most naval guns. Certainly some battleships carried larger guns than others – the largest being the 18-inch barrels carried on the two Japanese battleships of the Yamato class. In older ships, gun turrets were modified to permit greater elevation, which in turn helped increase the range of the guns. However, these improvements did little to alter the naval status quo. Essentially, all big guns relied on visual rangefinding, which limited the guns' effectiveness at night, or in poor visibility. Their fire control systems were certainly improvements on those fitted to the warships of World War I, but again these changes were incremental and evolutionary. Therefore they didn't significantly improve naval gunnery, save to make it more accurate. Radar though, would change all this.

The British were the first to introduce effective naval radar to ships. These earliest sets were air warning systems, designed to provide advance notice of imminent air attacks. Surface search radars were soon introduced, which allowed warships to detect enemy vessels regardless of the visibility conditions. These became increasingly sophisticated – for instance, by 1941 British surface search radars could detect the periscope of a submerged U-boat 5,000 yards away. As surface search radars improved, the next stage was to develop fire control radars linked to specific weapons. So, for instance, a fire control radar linked to the surface search radar could react to the sighting of an enemy warship, and the information would be passed to the ship's main guns, which could then fire at the target using the data provided by the radars. During the battle of North Cape in December 1943 the German battlecruiser *Scharnhorst* was engaged and sunk in poor visibility thanks to radar. The US Navy also made extensive use of radar, but while Germany and Japan developed their own radar systems, their performance was markedly inferior to those used by the Western Allies.

One area where guns developed extremely rapidly was the realm of anti-tank warfare. For the most part the tanks in use in 1918 were lumbering, unreliable contraptions, designed largely to cope with the difficult conditions of the shell-pocked battlefield. However, towards the end of the war the French developed light tanks which were both faster and better suited to operating in the terrain beyond the front lines, where they could exploit French breakthroughs. During the inter-war years these two approaches initially led to two different types of tank – the plodding infantry support version, which was the direct ancestor of the large and slow tanks used during the war, and light cruiser tanks, built for speed, following the example set by the French. Still, for the most part tanks remained relatively feeble and poorly armoured, and the light anti-tank guns developed during this period were able to deal with them. These had a calibre of around 37–40mm, firing a projectile weighing about 2 pounds. A prime example was the British 2-pounder, which in 1940 was used both as a tank gun and as Britain's main anti-tank gun.

By the summer of 1940 it had become clear that these guns couldn't knock out the latest generation of German tanks such as Panzer IIIs and Panzer IVs, except when firing at very close range. Similarly, the Germans encountered the same problem in Russia, when they first encountered the T-34 and the KV-1 – Soviet tanks which were largely immune to most German anti-tank guns. Clearly more powerful anti-tank guns were urgently needed. Most of the warring powers were working on the problem – it merely took the battles of 1940–41 to highlight the urgency. By the time the Germans invaded Russia, the 50-mm Pak38 was entering service, and it proved a useful stopgap until a more powerful anti-tank weapon could be developed. It was based on the 50-mm tank gun fitted to the Panzer III, and proved reasonably effective. However, the 75-mm Pak40, which entered service during the winter of 1941–42, proved a superb gun, both as an anti-tank weapon and as the main gun on tanks such as the Panzer IV. The Allies had to catch up fast, or risk losing the technological race.

Britain's answer was the Ordnance 6-pounder, a 57-mm gun which became the mainstay of the country's anti-tank batteries until the development of the far more powerful 17-pounder in late 1943. Still, the lighter and more manoeuvrable 6-pounder remained in use until the end of the war, its performance enhanced by better ammunition such as the armour-piercing rigid shell developed by the Americans, and the more effective armour-piercing discarding sabot round which was introduced before D-Day. The United States and the Soviet Union also developed their own 57-mm anti-tank guns, which in the case of the Soviets replaced an interim 45-mm M-42 model. Like its Soviet counterpart, the US 3-inch M5 appeared during 1943, but both guns were underpowered compared to the latest generation of German tanks such as the Panther and Tiger. The immediate solution was to provide these guns with improved ammunition, like those used by the British 6-pounder, but ultimately the answer was to build better anti-tank guns.

In tanks the need for bigger guns led to the Western Allied 75-mm and 76-mm guns, and the British 17-pounder, while the Soviets eventually upgraded their T-34 design to carry the 85-mm gun, rather than the 76.2-mm one, which had performed extremely well, but was hard-pressed to take on the new Tiger tank. Eventually, the Soviet 100-mm M-44 field gun would enter service in late 1944, which despite its name was an extremely powerful anti-tank weapon, used both in anti-tank batteries and in the SU-100 tank destroyer. This in turn was a counter to what was probably the best all-round anti-tank gun of the war, the German 88-mm. The 88-mm was designed during the 1930s as a heavy anti-aircraft gun, but its high muzzle velocity made it a superb light artillery piece, and, if provided with suitable ammunition, an anti-tank gun. This versatile weapon was then adapted into the Pak43, a dedicated anti-tank gun, which was also used in tank destroyers such as the Elefant, as well as the main tank gun used in Tiger tank. In whatever form it came in, the 'eighty-eight' was an extremely deadly weapon.

An interesting new development was the creation of the tapered bore anti-tank gun. This was a weapon that fired projectiles made from soft metal that would be deformed when they fired, so the projectile would pass through a barrel whose bore was actually smaller than the diameter of the shell. Clearly this was a difficult feat to accomplish, but if it worked the shell would have a greater velocity than if fired from a conventional gun barrel. This made the concept of a 'squeeze bore' or 'tapered bore' gun one that was particularly well-suited for anti-tank weapons.

The German ordnance designer Hermann Gerlich developed a 28-mm tapered-bore Pak41 anti-tank gun, which used a specially designed 40-mm round that was compressed as it passed through the gun's barrel. This weapon was designated as a light anti-tank rifle, and it proved moderately successful. Eventually the 75-mm Pak41 was introduced in limited numbers, which also operated on the Gerlich 'squeeze bore' principle, reducing the 75-mm shell to a higher-velocity 55-mm round. The Germans used tungsten for these 'squeeze bore' rounds, and eventually the shortage of this metal led to the abandonment of the project. The idea was resurrected by the Allies, but they produced no effective 'tapered bore' weapons before the end of the war.

Artillery tactics

The final area where artillery developed markedly during World War II was in the way the guns were employed on the battlefield. During World War I it was found that most indirect-fire missions were inflexible. Once the bombardment began it was almost impossible to change anything in response to developments on the ground. This was partly due to rigid planning, but also a problem of communication, as telephone lines would be cut by enemy shelling, or messengers lost before they could deliver verbal reports or instructions. During the inter-war period though, field radios became more reliable, and so forward observers or front-line commanders could now maintain workable communications with the guns.

During the previous war, the two main artillery missions were the barrage and the rolling barrage. The latter was simply a moving version of the former, timed to coincide with the pace of an infantry attack. Inevitably mistakes occurred, and the bombardment could fall short, or the timing would go awry, which in turn led to incidents of 'friendly fire'. Now, improved communications made it possible to vary the pace of a bombardment, or cease it completely if the circumstances warranted.

Predicted fire was a tactic developed after World War I to provide more flexibility on the battlefield. Fire missions could be pre-planned using ranging data or information taken from a map, and weather conditions factored in to make sure the shells landed on target. Then, when a target was selected, the guns could aim at the pre-arranged point using ranging data, and then open fire. This was used to harass enemy rear areas, to bombard enemy concentration areas, or just to shell enemy positions where activity was taking place, such as the relief of front-line units. The technique was used by all the major warring powers during the war.

Counter-battery fire had proved increasingly effective during World War I, thanks to flash spotting, or the use of sound ranging, where microphones recorded the time between a gun firing and the shells landing, and triangulated the results from several locations to produce an accurate location of the enemy battery. These techniques were improved between the wars, making counter-battery fire ever more effective.

The improvement of communications also created an opportunity for front-line units to obtain support from more than one friendly battery. Once guns were emplaced the locations of the batteries were surveyed and plotted. This allowed the fire of a number of batteries to be coordinated. While this had happened during the previous war, the use of the field radio permitted a single artillery observer to control the fire of a large number of guns.

A US Marine Corps 75mm M1 pack howitzer in action in the Pacific, 1944. (Stratford Archive)

All of this took time to arrange – normally it took up to three hours to prepare a barrage, and the more batteries that took part the longer the time needed to plan the mission. In a large bombardment, each battery had its own target area allocated to it, or a lane to advance up in the case of a rolling barrage. An variant of this was the artillery concentration, where all the batteries would fire at the same target area, saturating it with artillery fire. In the US Army this evolved into the 'Time on Target' mission, where several batteries timed their firing so that all of the shells landed on the target at the same moment. Guns could also be fired continually (known by the US Army as a 'Serenade'), or for a set number of rounds before either ceasing fire, or moving their bombardment to a different target area.

The British used the word 'stonk' as shorthand for a 'Standard Concentration' – a short sharp bombardment, usually called down at the request of an infantry commander from his supporting batteries. By providing his location as a map reference, and a bearing, or referring to a pre-arranged predicted fire location, the guns could then target the area very quickly, without having to wait for other batteries to coordinate their fire with them. It was even possible to coordinate these concentrations using all the batteries in a regiment, once the battery locations had been surveyed in. This was a more flexible way of providing defensive artillery support than anything available during the previous war. Similarly, guns were also used to lay barrages of smoke, to hide friendly troop movements from the enemy.

The massing of artillery fire was a technique that was particularly prized in the British army, after its development during the Western Desert campaign. From 1942 onwards, British artillery was able to concentrate all the guns in a division (usually three artillery regiments) in a bombardment, or even in predicted fire or concentration missions. This was known as an 'Uncle' mission'. Inevitably, this was developed further, allowing corps-sized 'Victor' missions, artillery group concentrations (known as 'Yoke' missions), or even army-sized fire concentrations, known as AGRA or 'William' missions. By contrast the Germans used more methodical procedures to provide map-based fire missions, which may have taken longer to set up, but they tended to be more accurate than the reactive missions undertaken by their Allied counterparts.

An American variant on the concentration as a form of reactive fire was the 'Zone and Sweep' mission. Here, when artillery support was requested by a forward observer or an infantry commander, the guns would concentrate on the target area, and then extend their fire to cover the surrounding area. This had the advantage of extending the 'beaten area' of the artillery concentration. For their part the Russians relied on massed bombardments and concentrations, at the expense of developing more reactive fire plans. Their effect though, was rendered devastating through sheer weight of fire. In all these circumstances, communications and plotting were the keys to accurate artillery fire. Only by plotting the location of friendly batteries and likely enemy targets could the guns properly coordinate their fire plans. As experience grew, this permitted ever larger fire concentrations to be planned. The real key though, was communications, linking a forward observer or infantry commander to a battery, and the batteries to each other by way of their own command structure. The result was a flexibility in the use of artillery which rendered it every bit as deadly a weapon as it had been during the previous global war.

Post-war developments

By the time the war ended in 1945 artillery had reached a peak of efficiency, both in terms of the development of the weapons themselves and in the way these guns were used. While there inevitably was a dramatic peacetime scaling back in military power, armies tended to retain their most efficient weapons, or rather those that fitted their new peacetime role. This meant for instance, that in the decades following the end of World War II the number of heavy weapons diminished, as the smaller armies, involved in smaller 'post-colonial' conflicts, needed light and rugged ordnance rather than cumbersome siege weapons. Only the continued possibility of another major war in Europe, fuelled by Cold War tensions, led to the retention of heavier artillery pieces, and the continued development of self-propelled guns.

The use of self-propelled guns, together with the virtually complete mechanisation of modern armies, was a response to the threat posed by nuclear weapons. From the 1950s onwards, tanks, armoured personnel carriers and self-propelled guns were all designed so they could be 'buttoned up' in the event of a strike by tactical nuclear weapons. This in theory would protect the crew, and allow them to continue fighting. So, the US M109 howitzer, the German PzH2000, the British AS90 and the Russian 2S19 Msta-S are all fully sealed self-propelled guns that have evolved from a range of earlier post-war designs. Unlike their predecessors though, these now incorporate sophisticated computerised gun laying, position-fixing and targeting systems, which make them far more efficient than their wartime predecessors. Nowadays, guns can move to a location and begin firing at a target within seconds, thanks to their computerised fire control systems.

Lighter towed guns are still of considerable use in smaller-scale conflicts, particularly those of 105-mm calibre or less. During the Vietnam War US towed howitzers were deployed in fire bases to cover the surrounding area of jungle, while in subsequent wars lighter guns were used to support troops operating in rugged terrain. A prime example was their use in the Falklands War of 1982, when the L118 105-mm light field howitzer was towed into action, or airlifted using helicopters during the advance on Port Stanley. Once in position these guns bombarded Argentinean positions in the mountains to the west of the town, before the defenders were assaulted by British ground troops.

A number of wartime developments continued after the end of hostilities, ushering in a number of post-war weapons systems ranging from rockets to superguns, recoilless rifles and automated anti-aircraft systems. The recoilless rifle was developed during the 1950s and 1960s using the wartime groundwork carried out on tapered bore weapons. These guns worked on the principle that two weapons back to back would have no recoil, as the forces of the blast would cancel each other out. So, a recoilless rifle was primarily an anti-tank weapon that used this principle to obviate the need for a heavy gun carriage. While this allowed the weapons to be mounted safely in vehicles, or carried by soldiers on foot, their main drawback was the excessive back-blast when the weapon was fired, which gave away the firer's position. Larger recoilless rifles fell into disuse, but weapons based on their principles are still used today, most notably the Carl Gustav portable anti-tank gun.

The great siege guns of the two world wars were effectively replaced by the use of guided weapons, usually launched from aircraft. However, in the 1980s the Iraqis developed a 'super gun' using the same principles, in a project codenamed Operation *Babylon*. The weapon was produced by the Canadian-born designer Gerald Bull, and had a bore of 350 mm (13.8 inches), with a total barrel length of 46 metres (151 feet). This was the prototype – Bell's real gun was to be 100 metres (300 feet) long, with a bore size of 1 metre (3.3 feet). However, he was assassinated before the weapon was finished, and parts being built overseas were impounded. The Iraqi 'super gun' was reportedly built to fire shells at Israel. By firing into the troposphere – the lowest portion of the earth's atmosphere – its shells could theoretically attain a range of over 1,000 kilometres (625 miles), thereby placing Israel with range of the weapon. The experiment died with its designer.

Computerised fire systems have transformed the use of light shipborne guns and anti-aircraft systems. However, belt-fed small guns and fully automated guns of under 150-mm calibre have been staples of naval warfare since the 1960s. Even here, most anti-aircraft and anti-ship weapons became the preserve of guided missiles, and naval artillery – like its land-based counterpart – was reduced to a fairly limited role of bombardment fire missions. However, an anti-ship capability remains, augmented by the latest computer guidance systems. Technologically, artillery had come a long way since 1945, but its use has also been curtailed dramatically. Anti-aircraft and anti-tank guns have been replaced by missile systems, and many old larger staples of the artillery world – siege guns, coastal artillery and even large howitzers – are no longer required. However, artillery is still needed on the modern battlefield, and arguably the sophistication of its modern fire control systems make it a far more deadly weapon than at any time in its history. However, its basic role – pounding a target with a heavy concentration of fire – has remained largely unchanged for more than 500 years. One suspects artillery will remain a military staple for many years to come.

FIGHTER ACES

KNIGHTS OF THE SKY

JOHN SADLER AND ROSIE SERDIVILLE

- -

Just over a decade after the first successful powered flight, fearless pioneers were flying over the battlefields of France in flimsy biplanes. As more aircraft took to the skies, their pilots began to develop tactics to take down enemy aviators. Though the infantry in their muddy trenches might see aerial combat as glorious and chivalric, the reality for these 'Knights of the Sky' was very different and undeniably deadly: new Royal Flying Corps subalterns in 1917 had a life expectancy of 11 days.

In 1915 the term 'ace' was coined to denote a pilot adept at downing enemy aircraft, and top aces like the Red Baron, René Fonck and Billy Bishop became household names. The idea of the ace continued after the 1918 Armistice, although as the size of air forces increased, the prominence of the ace diminished. But still, the pilots who swirled and danced in Hurricanes and Spitfires over southern England in 1940 were, and remain, feted as 'the Few' who stood between Britain and invasion. Flying aircraft advanced beyond the wildest dreams of Great War pilots, the 'top' fighter aces of World War II would accrue hundreds of kills, though their life expectancy was still measured in weeks, rather than years.

World War II cemented the vital role of air power, and post-war innovation gave fighter pilots jet-powered fighters, enabling them to pursue duels over huge areas above modern battlefields. This entertaining introduction explores the history and cult of the fighter ace from the first pilots through late 20th century conflicts, which leads to discussion of whether the era of the fighter ace is at an end.

ISBN 9781612004822 • £7.99 • $12.95

SHARPSHOOTERS

MARKSMEN THROUGH THE AGES

GARY YEE

- -◗

Throughout history, the best marksmen in any military force have been employed as marksmen or sharpshooters, and equipped with the best available weapons. The German states made the first serious use of sharpshooters on the battlefield during the Seven Years' War in the 18th century. Some of these talented riflemen were then employed as mercenaries in America, where the tactical use of the rifle in wooded terrain was valued.

By the Revolutionary Wars, American riflemen were formidable, able to blend into the landscape and take out targets at long range. Their potential was noted by the British who began to train rifle units; during the Napoleonic Wars, the Green Jackets were the elite of the British army. The mid-19th century saw the development of optical sights, meaning that the units of sharpshooters raised in the Civil War were even more lethal.

The accuracy of German sniper fire in the trenches in World War I provoked the British Army to create sniper schools, manuals, and counter-sniping tactics. However, lessons were not learned and the outbreak of World War II saw almost all major powers unprepared for sniping or counter-sniping, meaning that talented marksmen like Simö Häyhä were able to accrue massive scores.

In this accessible introduction packed with first-hand accounts, sniping expert Gary Yee explores the history of the marksman, his weapons, and tactics from the flintlock era through to the present day.

ISBN 9781612004860 • £7.99 • $12.95

GLADIATORS

FIGHTING TO THE DEATH IN ANCIENT ROME | M. C. BISHOP

This expert introduction explores the world of the gladiator in Ancient Rome: their weapons, fighting techniques and armour. The cult of the gladiator is explored, alongside their less glamorous fates which more often than not ended in violent death.

ISBN 9781612005133 • £7.99 • $12.95

VIKINGS

RAIDERS FROM THE SEA | KIM HJARDAR

Viking raiders were feared across Europe for centuries, striking suddenly and attacking with great force before withdrawing with stolen goods or captives. Viking society was highly militarised, honour was everything and losing one's reputation was worse than death. This short history of the Vikings discusses their ships, weapons and armour, and unique way of life.

ISBN 9781612005195 • £7.99 • $12.95

Knights

CHIVALRY AND VIOLENCE | JOHN SADLER AND ROSIE SERDIVILLE

A short introduction to the world of the medieval knight, from the years of training and the weapons he fought with, to the tournaments and culture surrounding the knightly life.

ISBN 9781612005171 • £7.99 • $12.95

GREEK WARRIORS

HOPLITES AND HEROES | CAROLYN WILLEKES

Thermopylae, Marathon: though fought 2,500 years ago in Ancient Greece, the names of these battles are more familiar to many than battles fought in the last half-century, but our concept of the men who fought in these battles may be more a product of Hollywood than Greece. This book sketches the change from heroic to hoplite warfare, and discusses the life, equipment and training of both the citizen soldiers of most Greek cities, and the professional soldiers of Sparta.

ISBN 9781612005157 • £7.99 • $12.95